ANNETTE

AND

SYLVIE

Being Volume One of

The Soul Enchanted

By

ROMAIN ROLLAND

Translated from the French by
BEN RAY REDMAN

NEW YORK
HENRY HOLT AND COMPANY
1925

Annette and Sylvie is the prelude of a work in several volumes, that bears the title: *The Soul Enchanted*.

Love, the first born of creatures,
Love, who later shall engender Thought. . . .

RIG-VEDA.

FOREWORD

Upon the threshold of a new journey which, without being as long as that of "Jean-Christophe," will include more than one stage, I would remind my readers of the friendly prayer which I addressed to them at a turning-point in the story of my musician. At the commencement of *Revolt*, I admonished them to consider each volume as one chapter of a moving work, whose thought unrolled only as rapidly as the life represented. Citing the old adage, *La fin loue la vie, et le soir le jour*, I added: When we shall have made an end, you may judge the worth of our effort.

Of course, I understand that each volume has its own character, that it must be judged separately as a work of art; but it would be premature to judge the general thought from a single volume. When I write a novel, I choose a human being with whom I feel certain affinities,—or, rather, it is he who chooses me. Once this person has been selected, I leave him perfectly free, I beware of mingling my personality with his. It is a weighty burden, a personality that one has borne for more than half a century. The divine boon of art is to deliver us from this burden, by giving us other souls to quaff, other lives to assume—(our Indian friends would say, "other of *our* lives"; for all is in each . . .).

So, when I have once adopted Jean-Christophe, or Colas, or Annette Rivière, I am no more than the secretary of their thoughts. I listen to them, I see them act, I see through their eyes. In the measure that they come to know their own hearts and men, I learn with them; when they make mistakes, I stumble; when they recover themselves, I pick myself up, and we set off again upon the road. I do not say that this road is the best. But this road is ours. Whether or not Christophe, Colas and Annette are right, Christophe, Colas and Annette are. Life is not the least of justifications.

Seek here neither thesis nor theory. Behold in this work merely the inner history of a life that is sincere, long, fertile in joys and sorrows, not exempt from contradictions, abounding in errors, yet always struggling to attain, in default of inaccessible Truth, that harmony of spirit which is our supreme truth.

R. R.

August, 1922.

ANNETTE AND SYLVIE

PART ONE

I

SHE was seated beside the window, with her back turned to the light, so that the rays of the setting sun fell upon the firm column of her neck. She had just come indoors. For the first time in months, Annette had spent the day in the open, tramping and finding intoxication in the spring sunlight. Tipsy sunlight, like pure wine, diluted by no shadow of leafless trees, and brightened by the cool air of the winter that had flown. Her head was humming, her veins pulsing, and her eyes were drenched in torrents of light. Red and gold beneath her closed eyelids. Gold and red in her body. Immobile, bemused, upon her chair, for an instant she lost consciousness. . . .

A pool, in the midst of woods, with a patch of sunlight like an eye. Around about, a circle of trees, their trunks befurred with

moss. She must bathe her body; she finds
herself undressed. The icy hand of the
water rubs her feet and knees. Voluptuous
torpor. In the pool of red and gold she
contemplates her nudity. . . . A feeling of
shame, obscure and indefinable, as though
other spying eyes were watching her. To
escape them she advances further into the
water, which rises to her chin. The sinuous
water becomes a living embrace; and slippery
creepers twine themselves about her legs.
She seeks to free herself, she sinks into the
slime. Above, the patch of sunlight sleeps
upon the pool. Angrily she thrusts her foot
against the bottom and rises to the surface.
The water now is gray, dull, and muddied;
but still the sunlight on its gleaming surface. . . . Annette grasps a willow branch
that overhangs the pool, to lift herself free
from the watery contamination. The leafy
limb covers her naked back and shoulders
like a wing. The shadow of night falls,
and the air is chill upon her neck. . . .

She emerges from her trance; only a few
moments have flown since she sank into it.

The sun is disappearing behind the hills of
Saint-Cloud. The cool of evening has come.

Sobered, Annette rises, shivering a little;
and, wrinkling her brows in irritation at
the lapse she has allowed herself, she goes
to sit down before the fire, within the
depths of her room. It is a pleasant wood
fire, designed to distract the eye and to
furnish company rather than to give
warmth; for from the garden, through
the open window, with the damp breeze
of an early spring evening, there enters the
melodious chattering of homing birds set-
tling down to sleep. Annette dreams; but
this time her eyes are open. She has recovered a foothold in her accustomed world.
She is in her own house: she is Annette
Rivière. And, as she leans towards the
flame that reddens her youthful face, teas-
ing with her foot the black cat that
stretches out its gold-barred belly, she once
more becomes conscious of her sorrow, that
for an instant had been forgotten; she re-
calls the image (escaped from her heart)
of the person she has lost. In deep mourn-
ing, with the trace of grief's passage not

yet effaced from her brow or from the
corners of her mouth, with her lower lids
still slightly swollen from recent tears; but
healthy, fresh, and bathed in sap like
youthful nature itself, this vigorous young
girl who is not beautiful but well made—
with heavy chestnut hair, lightly tanned
neck, starry eyes and flower-like cheeks—
seeking to enfold anew her wandering
glance and round shoulders in the dispersed
veils of her melancholy—this girl, sitting
thus, seems like a young widow watching
the departure of the beloved shade.

Widow, indeed, Annette was in her
heart; but he whose shade her fingers
sought to detain was her father.

Six months had passed already since she
had lost him. Towards the end of autumn,
Raoul Rivière, still young (he was not
quite fifty), had been carried off in two
days by an attack of uremia. Although
for several years he had been obliged to
show some consideration for the health he
had abused, he had not expected so brusque
a lowering of the curtain. He was a
Parisian architect, an old student of the

Villa Romaine, handsome, congenitally cunning and possessed of inordinate desires, lionized in drawing-rooms and honored by the official world; and all his life long he had known how to collect commissions, honors and windfalls without ever appearing to seek them. His was a typically Parisian face, popularized by photographs, magazine sketches and caricatures,—with bulging forehead, swelling at the temples, head lowered like a charging bull; round, protuberant eyes with an audacious glance; white bushy hair cut in a brush, and a little tuft of hair below his laughing, voracious mouth; the whole expression being marked by wit, insolence, charm, and effrontery. In the Parisian world of arts and pleasures, he was known by everyone. And yet none knew him. He was a man of dual nature, who knew admirably how to adapt himself to society for the sake of exploiting it; but he also knew how to conduct his hidden life as a thing apart. He was a man of strong passions and powerful vices who managed to cultivate them all, while taking care to reveal nothing that

might scare away his clients; he had his
secret museum (*fas ac nefas*), but only the
rarest initiates were allowed a glimpse of
it; he cared not a hang for public taste
and morality, but at the same time he con-
formed to them in his outward life and in
his official works.   There was none who
knew him, neither among his friends nor
among his enemies. .. . . His enemies? He
had none. Rivals at the most, who had
smarted that he might forge ahead.   But
they bore him no malice: having got the
better of them, he was such an adept at
the art of wheedling that they almost
smiled and begged his pardon, like those
timid persons on whose feet one treads.
Hard and cunning as he was, he had accomplished the feat of remaining on good
terms with the competitors he supplanted,
and with the women he abandoned.

In his own household he had been somewhat less fortunate. His wife had had the
bad taste to suffer from his infidelities.
Although it seemed to him that she should
have had ample time, during the twenty-
five years of their married life, to habituate

herself to them, she never learned resignation. Morosely virtuous, with a manner slightly cold as was her Lyonnaise beauty, possessed of feelings that were strong but concentrated, she lacked all adroitness in holding him; and she had still less of that eminently practical talent of ignoring what she could not help. She was too self-respecting to complain, yet she could not resign herself to hiding from him the fact that she knew and suffered. As he was sensitive (at least he believed he was) he avoided thinking of this; but he bore her a grudge for not knowing better how to veil her egotism. For some years they had lived practically apart; but by tacit accord they hid this from the eyes of the world, and even from their daughter, Annette, who never became cognizant of the situation. She had not sought to fathom her parents' misunderstanding; it was distasteful to her. And adolescence has enough preoccupations of its own. A fig for those of others! . . .

Raoul Rivière's cleverest act was winning his daughter to his side. Naturally,

he made no move in this direction; it was
a triumph of art. Not a word of reproach,
not an allusion to the wounds inflicted by
Madame Rivière; he was chivalrous, he
left his daughter to find out these things
for herself. Nor did she fail to do so, for
she too was under her father's spell. And
how could she fail to decide against the
woman who, being his wife, was clumsy
enough to spoil their happiness! In this
unequal battle poor Madame Rivière was
beaten in advance; and she crowned her
defeat by being the first to die. Raoul remained sole master of the field,—and of
his daughter's heart. For the past five
years Annette had lived morally enveloped
by her amiable father who was devoted to
her, and who, intending no harm, lavished
on her those charms that were natural to
him. His generosity to her was aug-
mented when he found less opportunity to
employ these charms outside; for during
the last two years he was kept closer to
home by warnings of the illness that was
to carry him off.

Nothing, then, had troubled the warm

intimacy that united father and daughter,
and filled Annette's unawakened heart.
She was between twenty-three and twenty-
four, but her heart seemed younger; its
development had not been forced. Perhaps, like all those who have a long future
before them, and because she felt a profound life pulsing within her, she let that
life amass itself, in no hurry to take stock
of it.

She took after both her parents: from
her father she came by the outline of her
features and the charming smile, which in
his case promised more than he realized,
and in hers, as she was still pure, more
than she wished; while from her mother
she inherited a surface tranquillity, a poise
of manner, and a mind that was serious
despite its extreme freedom. Doubly allur-
ing she was, with the charm of the one and
the reserve of the other. It was impossible
to guess which of the two temperaments
was dominant in her. Her true nature
still remained unknown,—to herself as well
as to others. None suspected her hidden
universe. She was an Eve in the garden,

half slumbering.   She had not yet become
conscious of the desires that were within
her; nothing had awakened them, for nothing had disturbed them.   It seemed that
she had but to stretch out her arm to
gather them.   She never tried, lulled by
their happy humming.   Perhaps she did
not wish to try. . . . Who knows how far
one tries to dupe oneself?   One would
rather not see the disturbing things within
one. . . . And she preferred to ignore that
interior sea.   The Annette whom people
knew, the Annette who knew herself, was
a very calm, reasonable, well-regulated little person, mistress of herself, who had
her own will and her own independent
judgment, but who, so far, had never had
occasion to oppose these to the established
rules of the world or of her household.

Without in any way neglecting the duties
of social life, nor being indifferent to its
pleasures, which she enjoyed with a healthy
appetite, she had felt the need of a more
serious activity.   She busied herself with
fairly thorough studies, with following
university courses, with passing examina-

tions and taking a double degree. Possessed of a lively intelligence that demanded occupation, she loved exact studies,
particularly the sciences, in which she was
highly gifted. Perhaps it was that her
healthy nature, with an instinct for equilibrium, felt the necessity of opposing the
strict discipline of a clear method and
sharply defined ideas to the disquieting attraction of that inner life which she feared
to face, and which, despite her precautions,
came beating on her door at each halt of
the inactive mind. This clear, accurate,
regular activity satisfied her for the moment. She did not care to speculate on
what would follow. Marriage held no
attraction for her; she avoided thought of
it. Her father smiled at her resolutions;
but he was disinclined to oppose them, for
he found them to his own advantage.

II

The disappearance of Raoul Rivière shook to its foundations the well-ordered edifice of which, without Annette's realizing it, he was the principal pillar. She was not unfamiliar with the face of death. Five years before she had made its acquaintance, when her mother had left her. But the features of this face are not always the same. After spending several months in a private hospital, Madame Rivière had departed silently, as she had lived, guarding the secret of her last terrors as she had the trials of her life; leaving behind her, in the candid egotism of the young girl, along with a gentle sorrow that resembled the first rains of spring, an impression of relief that was unconfessed, and the shadow of a remorse that was soon to be lost in the joy of living.

Quite different was the end of Raoul Rivière. Stricken in the midst of a happiness that he felt sure of enjoying for a

long time still, he brought to his departure
no philosophy. He greeted his sufferings
and the approach of death with cries of
revolt. Until the supreme breath of a gasping agony, like that of a galloping horse
that climbs a slope, he battled fearfully.
Those frightful images were stamped in
Annette's burning brain as though in wax.
She remained haunted by them at night.
In the darkness of her room, in bed, upon
the verge of sleep or suddenly awakening,
she revived the agony and the face of the
dying man with such violence that she
was the dying man himself: her eyes were
his eyes, her breath was *his* breath; she no
longer distinguished between them; in the
eye-sockets she recognized the appeal of a
drowning glance. She came close to de-
struction; but robust youth enjoys such
elasticity! The more the cord is stretched,
the further flies the arrow of life. The
blinding light of those maddening images
was extinguished by its own excess, and
night fell upon the memory. The features, the voice, the radiance of the vanished man, all had vanished: Annette, de-

termined to exhaust the shadow that was within her, could find no further trace of it. Nothing but herself. She alone. . . . Alone. The Eve of the garden was awakening without the companion at her side,—the man whom she had always felt near her, without seeking to define him; the man who, unknown to her and as yet indistinctly, was assuming the shape of love. And suddenly the garden lost its security. Disquieting breaths from without had entered it; both the breath of death and the breath of life. Annette opened her eyes, as did the world's first men at night, with the apprehension of a thousand unknown dangers ambushed about her, with the instinct of imminent battle. Of a sudden the dormant energies gathered themselves together, and held themselves tensely ready. And her solitude was peopled by passionate forces.

Her equilibrium was destroyed. Her studies, her work, now meant nothing to her; the place that she had accorded them in her life now seemed a mockery. But the other part of her life, which sorrow

had just touched, revealed itself to be of
immeasurable extent. The shock of the
injury had awakened all its fibres: around
the wound, opened by the disappearance
of the beloved companion, gathered all the
forces of love, hidden and unknown;
sucked in by the void that had been hollowed out, they came hastening from the
distant depths of her being. Surprised by
this invasion, Annette strove to evade its
significance; she persisted in relating everything to the precise object of her grief:
everything,—the sharp, burning stimulus
of Nature, whose spring breezes bathed her
in moisture; the vague and violent longing
for happiness . . . lost or desired?—the
arms outstretched towards the absent one;
and the bounding heart which yearned for
the past . . . or was it the future? But
she succeeded only in dissolving her grief
into a confused mystery of sorrow, passion,
and obscure pleasure. By this she was at
once devoured and revolted. . . .

On this evening in late April, she was
swept away by revolt. Her rational mind

waxed furious at the confused reveries which it had too long left uncontrolled, and of which it saw the danger. It wished to repel them, but this was not easy; they no longer listened; the mind had lost its habit of command. . . . Annette, tearing herself away from contemplation of the fire upon the hearth, from the insidious advance of the night that had completely fallen, stood up, chilly now, and, enveloping herself in a dressing-gown of her father's, she flooded the room with light.

It was Raoul Rivière's old study. Through the open bay-windows, through the sparse young foliage of the trees, one could see the Seine in the darkness, and on its sombre, seemingly immobile mass, the reflections of houses whose windows were being lighted upon the opposite bank, and of the daylight that was dying above the hills of Saint-Cloud. Raoul Rivière, who was a man of taste—although disinclined to use it to satisfy the insipid routine or laughable caprices of his wealthy clients— had chosen for himself, at the gates of Paris, on the Quai de Boulogne, an old

Louis XVI mansion that he had had no
hand in building. He had contented himself with making it comfortable. His
study had also served him admirably for
affairs of gallantry, and there was reason
to believe that the room had not suffered
from lack of use in this capacity. Here
Rivière had received more than one amiable visit, suspected by no one; for the
chamber had its private entrance from the
garden. But for two years the entrance
had been useless, and the sole feminine
visitor had been Annette. Annette, coming
and going, tidying things, pouring water
into a vase of flowers, constantly moving
about; then suddenly motionless over a
book, curled up in her favorite corner of
the divan, whence she might silently watch
the passage of the sinuous river and, without interrupting her absent-minded reading, carry on an absent-minded conversation with her father. But he, sitting
yonder, listless and weary, his sly profile
catching her slightest movement from the
corner of one eye; he, an old spoiled child
who could never admit that, wherever he

might be, he was not the center of all thoughts, harassed her with witticisms, wheedling questions, insistent, disturbing, in order to attract Annette's attention to himself and make sure that she was really listening to everything. . . . To the very end, touched and delighted that he could not do without her, she gave up everything else for the sake of devoting herself to him alone. Then he was satisfied; and, sure of his public, he showered upon it the resources of his brilliant mind. He shot off his rockets, he laid bare his memories. Of course, he was careful to select only the most flattering; and he arranged them *ad usum Delphini,* to the taste of the *dauphine,* cleverly guessing at her secret curiosities and her sudden fits of bristling repugnance. He told her precisely what she desired to hear; and Annette, all ears, was proud of his confidences. She was quite ready to believe that she possessed more of her father than her mother had ever known. Of his intimate life's story she remained, so she thought, the sole trustee.

But, since her father's death, another
trust had been left in her hands: all his
papers. Annette had no desire to learn
what they contained. Her piety told her
that they did not belong to her; but another sentiment whispered the contrary.
In any event, it was necessary to decide
upon their fate: Annette, sole heiress,
might die in her turn, and those family
papers should not be allowed to fall into
strange hands. It was urgent, then, to
examine them, and to determine whether
they were to be destroyed or preserved.
For some days now Annette had been decided on this course. But when she found
herself again, at evening, in the room that
was permeated by the beloved presence,
she lacked courage to do more than drink
in this presence for hours, without stirring. She feared, in opening these letters
of the past, too direct a contact with
reality.

Yet it must be done. This evening she
was resolved upon it. In the diffused
softness of this over tender night, in which
she disturbedly felt the dwindling of her

grief, she wished to affirm her possession of the dead man. She went toward the piece of rosewood furniture, more suitable for a coquette than for a worker, a high Louis XV chiffonier, in which Rivière had heaped his letters and intimate papers, disposing them in the seven or eight drawers that made the piece a kind of anticipatory and charming model of the American skyscraper. Annette, kneeling, pulled out the lower drawer; then to examine it the better, she lifted it out completely, and, returning to her place by the fire, she sank to her knees and bent over it. Not a sound in the house. She was living there alone, save for an old aunt who kept house and who scarcely counted: Aunt Victorine, an eclipsed sister of Annette's father, who had always lived to serve Rivière, and who now continued as housekeeper in the service of her niece,—not unlike an old cat, having finally become a part of the furniture of the house, to which she was as much attached, no doubt, as to the human beings. Having retired to her room early in the evening, her distant presence on the floor above, the peaceable coming and going of her old felt-shod feet, disturbed Annette's reveries no more than would a familiar animal.

She began to read, curious and a little troubled. But her orderly instinct and her need of calm, which insisted that everything in and around herself should be clearly arranged, imposed on her, as she picked up and unfolded the letters, a slowness of movement and a detached coldness that succeeded in deluding her for a time at least.

The first letters that she read were from her mother. The fretful tone at first called to mind her earlier impressions, not always kindly, sometimes a little irritated, mixed with some pity for what she had considered, from the height of her reason, a really unhealthy habit of mind: "Poor mama! . . ." But little by little, as she continued her reading, she perceived for the first time that this mental state was not without its causes. Certain allusions to Raoul's infidelities disturbed her. Too partial to pass judgment against her father, she hurried on, pretending that she had not clearly understood. Her filial piety furnished her excellent reasons for averting her eyes. But at the same time she discovered Madame Rivière's earnestness, her wounded tenderness, and she reproached herself for having misunderstood her, and having thus added to the sorrows of this martyr's life.

In the same drawer, side by side, reposed other bundles of letters (some even detached and mingled with her mother's) which Raoul's casual carelessness had jumbled together, as he had done with the correspondents themselves during his life of multiple households.

This time Annette's determined calm was subjected to a difficult test. From every sheet of the new bundle, voices spoke, much more intimate and surer of their power than that of poor Madame Rivière: they affirmed their proprietary rights over Raoul. Annette was revolted by them. Her first movement was to crumple in her hand the letters that she held, and throw them into the fire. But she snatched them out again.

Hesitantly she regarded the sheets, already seared by the flame, that she had rescued. It was certain that if she had had sound reasons, a moment ago, for not wishing to delve into her parents' quarrels, she now had still better ones for wishing to know nothing of her father's liaisons. But these reasons counted for nothing, now. She felt herself personally attacked. On what grounds, how or why, she could not have said. Bent over, motionless, wrinkling the end of her nose, her face pushed forward in a disgusted pout, like an irritated cat, she trembled with desire to throw back into the fire the insolent papers that she clutched in her fist. But, as her fingers loosened their hold, she could not resist the temptation of glancing at them. And then, suddenly decided, she opened her hand, unfolded the letters again, meticulously smoothing out with one finger the creases she had made. . . . And she read, —she read all.

III

With repulsion (and not without attraction, too) Annette witnessed the passage of those love affairs of which she had known nothing. They formed a motley and fantastic troop. In love as in art, Raoul's caprice was "period color." Annette recognized certain names belonging to her own world; and with hostility she recalled the smiles and caresses that she used to receive from certain favorites. Others belonged upon a less lofty social level; their spelling was no less free than the sentiments they expressed. Annette's disdainful pout was accentuated; but her mind, with sharp and mocking eyes like her father's, saw the comic aspect of these women who, leaning forward, with a wisp of hair in their eyes and the tip of their tongues thrust out, made their pens gallop over the paper. All these adventures, some a little longer, some a little shorter, but none very long after all, passed, succeeded one an-

other, and effaced one another. Annette
was grateful for that,—wounded, but disdainful.

She was not yet at the end of her dis-
coveries. In another drawer, sedulously
put apart (more carefully, she was forced
to remark, than her mother's letters) a new
bundle revealed a more enduring liaison.
Although the dates were carelessly indicated, it was easy to see that this correspondence embraced a long period of years.
It was in two handwritings: the one, in-
correct, slovenly, and backhand, stopped
half way through the packet; the other,
childish at first, gradually grew firmer, and
continued until the last years, even (and
this discovery was particularly painful to
Annette), up until the last months of her
father's life. And this correspondent, who
was robbing her of a part of that sacred
period of which she had thought herself
the unique possessor, this double intruder,
was addressing her father as "Father!"

She experienced the sensation of an intolerable wound. With an angry gesture
she flung her father's dressing-gown from

her shoulders. The letters fell from her hands, and she sank back in her chair with dry eyes and burning cheeks. She did not analyse her own emotions. She was too moved by passion to know what she thought. But, with all her passion, she was thinking: "He deceived me! . . ."

Again she picked up the hateful letters, and this time she did not let them go until she had absorbed them down to the very last line. She read, breathing deeply with her mouth shut, burned by a hidden fire of jealousy, and by another sentiment, still obscure, that had been awakened. Not for a second did the idea occur to her, in penetrating the intimacy of this correspondence, in possessing herself of her father's secrets, that she might be guilty of a moral misdemeanor. Not for a second did she doubt her right. . . . (Her right! The spirit of reason was far away; another power, a despotic one, was speaking!) . . . On the contrary, she felt that it was she who was wounded in her right—*in her right*—by her father!

She recovered herself, however. She

glimpsed, for an instant, the enormity of her pretension. What rights had she over him? What did he owe her? The imperious grumbling of passion answered: "Everything." Argument was useless! Annette, abandoned to her absurd resentment, suffered from the wound, and at the same time felt a bitter joy in those cruel forces that, for the first time, were thrusting their piercing goads into her flesh.

She spent a part of the night in reading. And when she finally went to bed, with her eyes closed she long continued to reread lines and words that made her start, until the deep sleep of youth overcame her, and she lay motionless, outstretched, breathing deeply, very calm, even relieved by the emotional expenditure that she had undergone.

She read again the next day; many times, during the days that followed, she reread the letters which never ceased to occupy her thoughts. Now she could almost reconstruct this life, this double life which had unrolled parallel to her own: the mother, a florist, whom Raoul had furnished funds to open a shop; the daughter, employed by a milliner, or perhaps a seamstress (it was not very clear). The one was named Delphine; and the other, the younger, Sylvie. To judge by their fantastic, negligent style of writing—a style that for all its carelessness was not lacking in charm—they resembled each other. Delphine seemed to have been a pleasant person who, despite a few little ruses that appeared here and there in her letters, could not have wearied Rivière very greatly with her demands. Neither the mother nor the daughter took life tragically. And besides, they seemed sure of Raoul's affection. It was perhaps the best way to conserve it. But this impertinent assurance ruffled Annette no less than did the extreme familiarity of their tone with him.

It was Sylvie who especially absorbed her jealous attention. The other had died, and Annette's pride affected to scorn the kind of intimacy that Delphine had enjoyed with her father; already she was forgetting that, a few days before, the discovery of similar attachments had been a sensible affront to her. Now that a much more profound intimacy had entered the lists, all other rivalries seemed negligible to her. With strained imagination she tried to picture to herself this stranger who, despite her ill will, was only half a stranger. The laughing ease, the calm familiarity of these letters in which Sylvie disposed of her father as though he were entirely her property, made Annette furious; she sought to outstare this insolent unknown so that she might confound her. But the little intruder defied her glance. She seemed to say: "It is my right: I am of *his* blood."

And the more irritated Annette became, the more this affirmation grew upon her. She fought against it too much not to gradually become accustomed to the combat, and even to the adversary. Finally, she could not get along without it. In the morning the first thought that greeted her upon awakening was of Sylvie; and now the sly voice of her rival said: "I am of *your* blood."

So clearly did she hear it, so vivid one

night was the vision of her unknown sister,
that Annette in her half-sleep stretched out
her arms to seize her.

And the next day, provoked, protesting,
but conquered, the desire held her and
would not let her go. She left the house,
in search of Sylvie.

IV

The address was in the letters. Annette
went to the Boulevard du Maine. It was
afternoon; Sylvie was at the work-shop.
Annette did not dare to hunt her out there.
She waited for a few days, and then went
back one evening after dinner. Sylvie had
not come in, or else she had already gone
out again; no one was quite sure. Annette,
who had been keyed up by nervous impa-·
tience for a whole day preceding each attempt, returned home disappointed; and a
secret cowardice advised her to give it up.
But she was one of those who never give
up anything on which they have once decided; they are all the less willing to yield
when the obstacle persists, or when they
are afraid of what may happen.

She went again, one day at the end of
May, towards nine in the evening. And
this time she was told that Sylvie was at
home. Six flights. She climbed too
quickly, for she did not wish to have time

to seek any reasons why she should turn back. At the top, her breath was short. She halted on the last stair. She did not know what she was going to find.

A long general hall, uncarpeted, tiled. At right and left, two doors ajar: voices called from one lodging to the other. Through the door on the left a reflection from the setting sun fell upon the red tiles. That was where Sylvie lived.

Annette knocked. Some one called out, "Come in!" without ceasing to chatter. Annette pushed open the door; the light from the golden heavens struck her full in the face. She saw a young girl, half-dressed, in a skirt, with bare shoulders, and bare feet thrust into red slippers, walking back and forth with her supple, plump back turned towards her. She was looking for something on her toilet table, talking to herself, and powdering her nose with a puff.

"Well now! What is it?" she demanded in a tone that was nasal because of the pins thrust in one corner of her mouth.

Then suddenly, distracted by a lilac
branch that was soaking in her water jug,
she plunged her nose into it with a grunt
of pleasure. Lifting her head, and looking into the mirror with her laughing eyes,
she caught sight of Annette behind her,
hesitating on the threshold, aureoled in
sunlight. "Oh!" she exclaimed, turned
around with bare arms lifted above her
head, quickly thrust the pins back into her
rearranged hair, came forward with hands
outstretched, and then suddenly withdrew
them, making a gesture of welcome that
was cordial but reserved. Annette entered,
vainly trying to speak. Sylvie was silent
too. She offered her visitor a chair, and
slipping into a well-worn, blue-striped
dressing-gown, she sat down on the bed opposite her. They looked at each other,
and each waited for the other to begin.

How different they were! Each studied
the other with sharp, precise, unindulgent
eyes which asked: "Who are you?"

Sylvie saw Annette, big, fresh, large of
face, her nose a little snubbed, her fore-

head like that of a young heifer beneath a
mass of twisted golden brown hair, with
very thick eyebrows, large clear blue eyes
that protruded a trifle, and that grew
strangely hard at times when waves of
emotion swept up from her heart; her
mouth was large and her lips firm, with a
light down at the corners, and habitually
closed in a defensive, watchful, determined pout,—but when they opened they
were illumined by a timid, radiant and
delightful smile which transformed her
whole countenance; her chin, like her
cheeks, was full but not fat, both solidly
cut; nape, neck and hands were the color
of dark honey; beneath her beautiful, firm
skin flowed pure blood. A little heavy of
figure, her bust a trifle square, she had
breasts that were large and full: Sylvie's
practised eye felt them under the dress,
lingering longest on the fine shoulders, so
perfectly proportioned that they formed,
with the white, round column of her neck,
Annette's greatest physical charm. She
knew how to dress, she was turned out

with care; an excessive, an over-studied care in Sylvie's opinion: hair well done, not a ringlet out of place, not a hook and eye at fault, everything in order. Sylvie was asking herself: "And is she the same inside?"

Annette saw Sylvie, almost as tall as herself (perhaps just as tall) but thin, slender of figure, with a head that was small for her body, now half-naked under her peignor, and a throat that was slight but plump, while her arms too were plump: balancing herself on her little rump, she sat with her hands clasped over her round knees. Round too were her forehead and her chin; her little nose turned up; her light brown hair grew low on the temples and curled over the cheeks, and little wandering hairs appeared on the nape and the white, very white and slender, neck. A hothouse plant. The two profiles of her face were asymmetrical: the right-hand one was languorous, sentimental,—a sleeping cat; the left-hand one, malicious, watchful,— a biting cat. When she spoke, her upper lip drew back over laughing teeth. And Annette was thinking: "Beware of her bite!"

How different they were! . . . And yet at the first glance both had recognized the expression, the clear eyes, the forehead, the wrinkle at the corner of the mouth,—the father. . . .

Annette, frightened and stiff, took her courage in her hands and, in a pale voice that was chilled by excess of emotion, she told who she was, her name. Sylvie let her speak without ceasing to stare at her; then, calmly, with a slightly cruel smile of her curled upper lip, she said: "I knew it."

Annette started.

"How?"

"I've seen you before, often, with father. . . ."

Before those last words there was an imperceptible hesitation. Perhaps she had been going to say "*my* father." But she felt an ironic pity for Annette's glance that read her lips. Annette understood, averted her eyes, and blushed, humiliated.

Sylvie missed none of it; she took a leisurely delight in Annette's embarrassment. She continued to speak without haste, studiedly. She said that she had been in the church, at the funeral service, in one of the aisles, and that she had seen everything. Her singsong, rather nasal voice reeled off her narrative with no show of emotion. But if Sylvie knew how to see, Annette knew how to hear; and when the girl had finished, Annette, raising her eyes, asked her:

"You loved him very much?"

The eyes of the two sisters exchanged a caress. But this lasted for a moment only. Already a jealous shadow had clouded Annette's expression, and she continued:

"He loved you very much."

She sincerely wished to please Sylvie, but she could not help a shade of spite creeping into her voice. Sylvie thought that she could sense a patronising tone. Immediately her paws showed their little claws, and she said spiritedly:

"Oh! yes, he loved me tremendously!"

She made a little pause; then, with a complacent air, let fly:

"And he was *very* fond of you, too. He often told me so."

Annette's passionate hands, her large nervous hands, trembled and clasped each other. Sylvie watched them. With contracted throat, Annette asked:

"He spoke to you of me, often?"

"Often," repeated the innocent Sylvie.

There was no assurance that she spoke the truth; but Annette, who had scant skill in hiding her own thoughts, did not suspect the words of others, and those of Sylvie touched her heart. . . . So, her father spoke of her to Sylvie, they talked about her together! And she, to the very last day, had known nothing; he had seemed to confide in her, and he had duped her; he had kept her out of things, she had not even known of her sister's existence! Such inequality, such injustice overwhelmed her. She felt that she was beaten. But she did not wish to show it; so she sought a weapon, found it, and said:

"You must have seen very little of him during the last years."

"Yes," conceded Sylvie regretfully, "during the last years that was so. He was sick. *They* kept him shut up."

There was a hostile silence. Both were smiling, both were champing at the bit: Annette, rigid and strained; Sylvie, her expression as false as a gambler's counter, caressing, mannered. Before going on with the game, they were counting up the points. Annette, a little relieved at having won a (very slight) advantage, and secretly ashamed of her evil thoughts, tried to put the conversation on a more cordial basis. She spoke of the desire she had felt to meet the girl in whom, too, her father lived again,—"*a little*." But it was in vain; despite herself she made it clear that there was a difference between their shares, and she let it be understood that hers was the privileged one. She told Sylvie about Raoul's last years, and she could not help showing how much *more* intimate she had been with him. Sylvie profited by a pause in the narrative to furnish Annette, in return, with her own memories of the paternal affection. And each, against her will, envied the other's share; and each tried to make her own seem the bigger. Speaking or listening (not wishing to listen, but hearing just the same) they continued to inspect each other from head to foot. Sylvie complaisantly compared her long legs, slim ankles and small bare feet, lost in their slippers, with Annette's somewhat heavy extremities and awkward ankles. And Annette, studying Sylvie's hands, did not fail to note the cultivated moons of the over-pink nails. It was not merely two young girls who confronted each other; it was two rival households. So, despite the apparent freedom of the conversation, they remained armed with eye and tongue, and observed each other harshly. The fierce sharpness of jealousy made each bluntly penetrate, at first glance, to the very depths of the other; to the faults and hidden vices unsuspected perhaps by their possessor. Sylvie recognized in Annette the demon of pride, inflexibility of prin-

ciple, despotic violence, which had not yet,
however, found occasion to exert itself.
Annette recognized in Sylvie a practised
sharpness and a smiling falseness. Later,
when they loved each other, they would
have given much to forget what they had
seen. But for the instant their animosity
gazed through a magnifying glass. There
were seconds when they hated each other.
Annette, with a bursting heart, was thinking:

"It isn't right, it isn't right! I should
set the example."

Her eyes made a tour of the modest
room, taking in the window, the lace curtains, the roof and chimneys of the opposite house under the moonlight, the lilac
branch in the broken water jug.

In a cold tone, colder for the fact that
she was burning inside, she offered Sylvie
her friendship, her assistance. . . . Sylvie,
negligently, with a malicious little smile,
listened, made no reply. . . . Annette,
mortified, ill hiding her piqued pride and
incipient passion, rose abruptly. They ex-

changed a pleasant, commonplace good-
bye. And, with sorrow and anger in her
heart, Annette went out.

But as she reached the end of the tiled
hall, and was already descending the first
step of the stairs, Sylvie came running towards her, in her little Turkish slippers,
one of which she lost on the way, and
from behind she slipped her arms around
Annette's neck. Annette turned, crying
out with emotion. She hugged Sylvie in
a burst of passion; and Sylvie cried out
too, but with laughter at the violence of
the embrace. Their mouths met ardently.
Loving words. Affectionate murmurs.
Thanks, promises that they would see each
other soon. . . .

They drew apart. Annette, laughing
with happiness, found that without realizing it she had descended to the bottom of
the staircase. From above she heard a
gamin's whistle, as though calling a dog,
and Sylvie's voice whispering:

"Annette!"

She raised her head and saw high above

her in a patch of light Sylvie's laughing face bending down.

"Catch!"

And Annette received full in her face a rain of drops and the wet lilac that Sylvie had thrown down to her, at the same time throwing kisses with both hands. . . .

Sylvie vanished. Annette, with lifted head, continued to look for her when she was no longer there. And, clasping the branch of wet flowers in her arms, she kissed the lilac.

V

Despite the distance, and although certain streets were not very safe at this belated hour, Annette returned home on foot. She could easily have danced. When she finally reached the house, happy and troubled, she did not retire until she had placed the flowers in a vase beside her bed. And then she got up again to take them out and put them in her water jug, as they had been at Sylvie's. In bed again, she kept her lamp lighted, for she did not wish to take leave of this day. But suddenly, three hours later, she awakened in the middle of the night. The flowers were really there; it had not been a dream, she had seen Sylvie. . . . She fell asleep again, upon the breast of that dear image.

The days that followed were filled by the buzzing of bees erecting a new hive. Just as a swarm groups itself around a young queen, so Annette constructed a new future around Sylvie. The old hive was deserted; its queen was indeed dead. Attempting to mask this revolution in the palace, the passionate heart pretended to believe that its love for the father had been transferred to Sylvie, and that it would rediscover him there. . . . But Annette really knew that she was bidding him farewell.

There sounded the imperious voice of new love, which creates and destroys. . . . Memories of the father were thrust, pitilessly, from view. Familiar objects were relegated to the pious shadow of rooms in which they ran no risk of being frequently disturbed. The greatcoat was thrust into the bottom of an old closet. Having put it away, Annette took it out again indecisively, pressed her cheek against it, then suddenly in anger thrust it from her. Illogicality of passion! Which of the two was the traitor? . . .

She was enamoured of the sister she had discovered. She scarcely knew her! But as soon as one loves, such an uncertainty is only an added attraction. The mystery of the unknown is added to the charm of

what one thinks one knows. Of the Sylvie
she had glimpsed, she wished to remember
only what had pleased her. Secretly she
admitted that this was not very exact; but
when she honestly sought to recall the
shadows of the portrait, she heard the
little slippers trotting down the hall, and
felt Sylvie's bare arms clasped about her
neck.

Sylvie was going to come. She had promised. . . . Annette was preparing everything for her reception. Where would she
put her? There, in her pretty room.
Sylvie would sit here, in her favorite place,
before the open window. In imagination
Annette saw everything through her sister's
eyes, and took delight in showing Sylvie
her house, her bibelots, her trees clothed
in their softest greenery, and the vista
yonder over the flowered hills. In sharing
with Sylvie the grace and comforts of her
life she enjoyed them with the freshness
of new sensations. But the thought occurred to her that Sylvie's eyes might draw
comparisons between her own lodging and
the Boulogne house. A shadow fell across

her joy. This inequality weighed upon
her, as though it had been her fault.
Couldn't she correct it by asking Sylvie to
share with her the advantages that fate
had given her? Yes, but this would be to
give her still another advantage. And Annette foresaw that she would not gain her
consent without a struggle. She remembered the mocking silence with which
Sylvie had greeted her first invitations.
Her sensitiveness would have to be hu-
mored. How could it be done? Annette
reviewed four or five plans in her mind.
None satisfied her. Ten times she changed
the arrangement of the room: after having
placed in it her most valuable possessions,
with a childish pleasure, she carried them
out again and left only the simplest things.
There was not a detail—a flower on the
landing, the place of a portrait—that she
did not argue over. . . . Sylvie must not
arrive before everything was in order! But
Sylvie was in no hurry, and Annette had
time to make and remake, again and again,
her little arrangements. She found Sylvie
very slow in coming, but she profited by

this to revise her plans. Unconscious comedy! She was deluding herself by attributing importance to these trifles. All this bustle of arrangement and rearrangement was only a pretext to distract her attention from another bustle of passionate thoughts which was troubling the habitual order of her rational life.

The pretext wore itself out. This time all was ready. And Sylvie did not come. In imagination Annette had already welcomed her ten times. She was exhausted with waiting. . . . Yet she could not go back to Sylvie's! What if, when she went to see her again, she should read in Sylvie's bored eyes that her sister could get along very well without her! At the very idea Annette's pride bled. No, rather than this humiliation, it would be better never to see her again! Yet . . . She decided hastily, and dressed herself to go in search of the forgetful girl. But she had not finished buttoning her gloves before she lost courage; and, with her legs sinking under her, she sat down on a chair in the vestibule, not knowing what to do. . . .

And just at that moment,—when Annette had sunk down beside the door, with her hat on her head, all ready to go out, yet not able to make up her mind,—just then, Sylvie rang the bell!

Between the sound of the bell and the opening of the door ten seconds did not elapse. Such promptness and the sight of Annette's delighted eyes were enough to tell Sylvie that she was expected. They were already kissing each other, standing on the door-sill, before a word was said. Then Annette impetuously dragged Sylvie through the house, without letting go of her hands, devouring her with her eyes, and laughing foolishly to herself like a happy child. . . .

And nothing happened as she had anticipated. Not one of the prepared phrases of welcome served. She did not seat Sylvie in the chosen place. Turning their backs to the window, they both sat on the divan, side by side, gazing into each other's eyes, speaking without listening; their expressions said:

Annette: "At last! You are really here?"

Sylvie: "You see, I've come. . . ."

But Sylvie, having examined Annette, said: "You were going out?"

Annette shook her head without wishing to explain. Sylvie understood perfectly and, leaning over, she whispered:

"You were coming to my place?"

Annette started and, resting her cheek on her sister's shoulder, she murmured: "Bad girl!"

"Why?" demanded Sylvie, kissing Annette's fair eyebrows with the corner of her mouth.

Annette did not reply. Sylvie knew the answer. She smiled, peeking maliciously at Annette who was now avoiding her glance. The violent girl! Her spirit was broken. A sudden timidity had fallen upon her, like a net. They sat without stirring, the big sister leaning on the shoulder of the little one, who was satisfied at having so promptly established her power. . . .

Then Annette raised her head and, both

mistresses of their first emotion, they began
to talk like old friends.

No longer were their intentions hostile.
On the contrary, each was desirous of sur-
rendering herself to the other. . . . Oh,
not completely, however! They knew that
there are things in every one which it does
not do to show. Even when one loves?
Precisely when one loves! But what
things, exactly? Each, while unbosoming
herself, kept her secrets, sounding out the
limits of what the other's love could bear.
And more than one confidence that began
frankly, oscillated uncertainly in the midst
of a phrase, and then ran prettily into a
little lie. They did not know each other;
in more than one respect they were disconcerting enigmas to each other: two natures,
two worlds, strangers in spite of all. For
this visit, Sylvie—she had thought about it
more than she would have admitted—had
made herself as lovely as possible. And her
possible was much. Annette was captured
by her charm and at the same time embarrassed by certain little artifices of coquetry
that made her uncomfortable. Sylvie per-

ceived this, without trying to change in any way; and she was at once attracted and intimidated by this big sister of hers who was so free and so naïve, so ardent and so reserved. (To hear her chatter one would not have suspected the intimidation!) Both were keen and extremely observant, and they missed not a wink nor a thought. They were not yet sure of each other. Suspicious and expansive, they wished to give themselves; yes, but they did not wish to give without receiving. Each was possessed by a devil of petty pride. Annette's was the stronger; but in her the forces of love, too, were stronger, and she betrayed herself. When she gave more than she had wished, it was a defeat that Sylvie relished. So the two negotiators, burning to understand each other, but wisely circumspect, testing each movement, advanced cautiously. . . .

The duel was an unfair one. Very quickly Sylvie became aware of Annette's imperious and imploring love. She saw it more clearly than Annette herself. She tested it; with sheathed claws she played with it, without seeming to do so. Annette felt that she was conquered. It caused her shame and joy.

At Sylvie's request she showed her all her rooms. She would not have done this on her own initiative; she was afraid to gall her sister by displaying the comfort in which she lived, but to her relief Sylvie manifested not the slightest pique. She was perfectly at her ease, coming and going, looking and touching, as though she were at home. It was Annette, in fact, who was disturbed by this perfect poise; and at the same time her affection rejoiced in it. Passing by her sister's bed, Sylvie gave the pillow a friendly little pat. Curiously she examined the toilet table, making an accurate survey of the bottles at a glance; went absent-mindedly into the library, enthused over a pair of curtains, criticised an arm-chair, tried another, poked her nose into a half-open cupboard, felt the silk of a dress; and, having made her tour, returned to Annette's bedroom where she sat down in the low armchair near the bed and went on with the conversation.

Annette offered her tea, to which Sylvie preferred two fingers of sugared wine. Sucking a biscuit with the end of her tongue, Sylvie looked at Annette who was hesitating, wishing to speak; and she wanted to say to her:

"Out with it then!"

Finally Annette plucked up courage, and with a brusqueness that was caused by her suppressed affection she proposed to Sylvie that she come to live with her. Sylvie smiled, did not speak, swallowed her mouthful, dipped her crumbs and fingers in her wine, smiled again prettily, thanking her sister with eyes and a full-mouth, shaking her head as one does when talking to a child. And then she said:

"Darling. . . ."

And she refused.

Annette insisted, pressing her; she tried to compel consent with an imperious violence. It was Sylvie's turn now not to wish to speak! She excused herself with half-words, in a caressing voice, slightly embarrassed and a little malicious as well. . . . (She was very fond of her big sister

who was so abrupt, tender, and frank!)
She said:

"I can't."

And Annette asked: "But why?"

And Sylvie replied: "I have a sweetheart."

For the space of a second Annette did
not understand. Then she understood only
too well, and she was dumbfounded.
Watching her from the corner of one eye,
Sylvie rose, still smiling, and left amid a
twittering of little words and kisses.

VI

Annette was left to contemplate her destroyed castle. She felt a great, confused pain composed of mingled feelings. Bitter ones there were in plenty, which she would rather not have recognized, but which spasmodically made her throat contract. . . . She who had thought herself free from prejudice; the idea that this pretty sister of hers. . . . Oh! it was too painful! She could have wept over it. . . . Why? It was stupid! Jealousy again? . . . No!

She shrugged her shoulders and stood up. She wished to think no more about it. . . . With long strides she went from room to room, seeking distraction. Then she realized that she was retracting her sister's promenade through the apartment. She could think only of her. Of her and that other . . . Jealous, decidedly? No! No! No! No! . . . She stamped her foot angrily. She would not admit it! . . . But, whether she admitted it or not, the

pain was gnawing at her heart. She sought
moral explanations; and she found them.
It was her purity that suffered. In her
complex nature, rich in contradictory instincts that had not yet had occasion to
conflict, there was no lack of puritanical
forces. Yet it was not religious scruples
that disturbed her. Brought up by a sceptical father and a free-thinking mother,
outside the pale of any church, she was
accustomed to discuss everything. She was
not afraid to submit any social prejudice
to the spirit of examination. She admitted
free love; in theory she admitted it readily.
Often in conversation with her father or
with fellow students she had upheld it,
and in this the juvenile desire to appear
"advanced" had played an unimportant
part; she sincerely thought that freedom
in love was legitimate, natural, and even
right. She had never thought of blaming
the pretty girls of Paris who lived as they
pleased; she regarded them sympathet-
ically, certainly with more sympathy than
the women of her middle-class world.
. . . Well then, what was it that hurt her

now?   Sylvie was exercising her right.
. . . Her right?   No, not her right!
Others, but not she!   One is lenient with
those one does not hold so high.   For her
sister as for herself Annette had, justly or
not—yes, justly!—very strict standards.
Love for one person only seemed to her
an aristocracy of the heart.   Sylvie had
fallen.   Annette blamed her for it!   "One
love only?   Love for you! . . . Jealous
girl, you are lying to yourself! . . ."   But
the more jealous she was of Sylvie, the
more she loved her; and the more irritated
she became with her, the more she loved
her.   One can be so greatly irritated only
by those one loves!

   Her little sister's charm was calmly
working.   It was useless to be annoyed, to
wish that she were different.   Little by
little, Annette became conscious of another
feeling: curiosity.   Despite herself, her
mind was trying to imagine Sylvie's mode
of life.   She thought about it entirely too
much.   She ended by putting herself in
Sylvie's place; and she was rather confused
to admit that she did not find it too bad. .

The scorn of herself, the indignant revolt that this produced, made her the more severe towards Sylvie. She continued to sulk, and forbade herself to visit her sister again.

Sylvie was not at all disturbed. That Annette gave no sign of life did not in any way trouble her. She had judged her big sister; she knew that Annette would come back. The period of waiting did not weigh upon her; she had enough to occupy her heart. First of all, her sweetheart, who occupied, nevertheless, only a corner of it, and that not for long. And there were so many other things! She loved Annette. But, after all, she had lived without her for almost twenty years. She could wait a few weeks more. . . . She imagined what was going on in her sister's mind. She found a certain amusement in this, mixed with a residue of hostility. Two rival races; two classes. When she had been at Annette's, Sylvie had compared their lives and conditions, although she had not appeared to do so. She was thinking:

"All the same, you see, we have our little advantages. I have what you haven't. . . . You thought that you could hold me, and you can't. Yes, go ahead, go ahead, pout and purse your lips! I have shocked your conventions. . . . What a blow, my poor Annette!"

And, laughing at the discomfiture which she imagined she read in Annette's face, she pressed her hand to her lips and threw a kiss. But, even while she told herself that Annette was suffering and that it was a bitter dose for her to swallow, she was not offended. And, as one does when a child balks before a full spoon, she whispered, slyly and cajolingly:

"Come on, my little one! Open your mouth! There you are!"

It was not merely a question of shocked conventions. Sylvie knew perfectly well that she had wounded Annette in another feeling much less easily confessed. And the little brigand was delighted at the thought, for it made her feel that she was her sister's mistress; she would make the most of it. . . . "Poor Annette! Can you fight against yourself!" Sylvie was sure, absolutely sure, that she would "have" her. Mocking, yet at the same time touched, she whispered to her in imagination.

"Go on! I won't take advantage of it. . . ."

She wouldn't take advantage of it? . . . And why not? It's amusing to take advantages. After all, life is war. To the victor are the spoils. If the vanquished consents, it's because it is to his advantage!

"Pshaw! We shall see!"

VII

One Monday morning Sylvie was doing
some errands, when she caught sight of
Annette, a little in front of her and
walking in the same direction, on the Rue
de Sèvres. She amused herself by following her for a time, so that she might observe her. Annette was walking with long
strides, as was her habit. Sylvie, whose
steps were short, quick, supple, dancing,
laughed at her boyish, athletic pace; but
she appreciated the beautiful harmony of
her vigorous body. Head held straight,
looking neither to right nor left, Annette
was absorbed. Sylvie caught up with her
and continued to walk beside her on the
sidewalk without Annette's noticing her.
Imitating her gait, and peeking from the
corner of one eye at her big sister's cheek,
which seemed paled by a melancholy
shadow, Sylvie moved her lips, without
turning her head, and said in a low voice:
"Annette. . . ."

It was impossible to hear in the noise of the street. Sylvie barely heard herself. Yet Annette heard. Or was it that she was conscious of this mocking "double" that had for some moments been silently escorting her? Suddenly she saw beside her the amused profile, the lips that moved comically without speaking, the little laughing eye with its sidewise glance. . . . Then she stopped, with one of those movements of impetuous joy that had already surprised and charmed Sylvie on one occasion. Abruptly she held out her arms. Her whole being quivered. Sylvie thought:

"She is going to spring. . . ."

For an instant only. Already she had recovered herself; and, almost coldly, she said:

"Good-morning, Sylvie."

But her cheeks were full of color, and her stiffness could not withstand the burst of laughter from the younger girl, who was delighted with her trick. Annette laughed with her:

"Oh! You've caught me!"

Sylvie took her arm, and they walked

on, considerately suiting their steps to each other.

"Were you there long?" asked Annette.

"Oh! about a half-hour," Sylvie affirmed unhesitatingly.

"No?" exclaimed the credulous Annette.

"I followed your movements. I saw everything. Everything. You talked as you walked."

"It's not true, it's not true," protested Annette. "What a little liar! . . ."

Their two arms tightened. They began to chatter about the errands they had just done. They were perfectly happy. In the midst of an impassioned account of a White Sale at the Bon Marché, where one had been and where the other was going, —in the uproar of a street that they were crossing, slipping between the vehicles with the sure instinct of two little Parisiennes, Sylvie murmured in Annette's ear:

"You haven't kissed me!"

Annette's quick movement nearly crushed her. As they approached the sidewalk, still walking, their lips met. . . . Hug-

ging each other closer, they were walking
now along a quieter street, that led . . .
Where did it lead? . . .

"Where are we going?"

They stopped, amused to find that in
the midst of their chattering they had lost
their way. Sylvie, clutching Annette, said:

"Let's lunch together."

Annette demurred, — (the unexpected
charmed her, but embarrassed her a little
too: she was methodical),—mentioning her
old aunt, who was waiting for her. But
Sylvie was not bothered by these trifling
details: she had got hold of Annette, and
she wasn't going to let her go. She made
her telephone her aunt from a public station, and led her to a creamery which she
knew. For the two young girls, and particularly for Annette, it was an outing, this
little luncheon to which Sylvie insisted on
treating her more fortunate sister. (Annette understood why.) Annette found
everything exquisite. She went into ecsta-
sies over the bread, over the well-done
cutlet. And, last of all, there were straw-

berries in cream on which they regaled themselves, licking them with their tongues.

But their tongues were even more occupied in talking than in eating. They spoke, however, of only insignificant things, drinking each other in, their eyes, their voices, and their radiance. Instinct has its roads, the shortest and the best. The time had not come to touch on essential subjects. They circled around, circled joyously, like those buzzing wasps that turn ten times around a plate before alighting. They did not alight. . . .

Sylvie stood up, and said: "Now it's time to go to work."

Annette assumed the dashed expression of a child abruptly robbed of its dessert, and exclaimed: "It has been so nice! I haven't had enough."

"Nor I," replied Sylvie, laughing. "When shall we do it again?"

"The sooner and the longer the better. . . . This ended too soon."

"This evening then. Meet me at the door of the shop at about six."

Annette was disconcerted.

"But shall we be alone?"

She was disturbed at the idea that she might meet "the other."

Sylvie read her meaning.

"Yes, yes, we shall be alone," she said indulgently, with an ironic emphasis. She calmly explained that her friend had gone to spend two or three days in the country with his family. Annette blushed when she saw that Sylvie had guessed; she did not remember that she had vowed, morning and evening, to give evidence of her moral disapprobation. So far as morality went, she now saw only one thing: "This evening *he* will not be there."

What happiness! They could spend the whole evening together.

She spoke her thought, clapping her hands. Sylvie balanced on one foot as though she were going to dance, grinned with pleasure, and said: "Everybody's happy." Then, as a man had just come into the shop, she assumed a genteel air, said, "Good-bye, my dear," and was off like a shot.

They met again, some hours later, at the exit of the frivolous swarm. Babbling, peering, trotting along, completing their hair-dressing before a pocket-mirror or before a stray looking-glass, the little seamstresses turned around as they passed and outstared Annette with their tired, sharp, curious eyes; then, ten steps further on, trotting, peering, babbling, they turned about to look at Sylvie who was kissing Annette. And Annette was pained to see that Sylvie had talked.

She took her sister to dine at Boulogne. Sylvie had invited herself. To spare the aunt, who would have exclaimed, "Oh!" and "Ah!" it was arranged on the way that Sylvie should be introduced as a friend. But this didn't prevent her, at the end of dinner, when the old lady was retiring to her own room, conquered by the charms of the little schemer, from calling her "Aunt" as though in familiar playfulness. . . .

Alone, in the great garden, by the light of a summer night. Tenderly intertwined, they walked with little steps, drinking in

the fragrance of the weary flowers, exhaled
at the close of a fine day. Like the flowers,
their souls exhaled their secrets. This time
Sylvie responded to Annette's questions,
hiding little. She told the story of her life
from infancy; and, first of all, her memories of her father. They spoke of him
now without embarrassment, and with no
mutual envy; he belonged to them both,
and they judged him with an indulgent,
ironic smile, as a big, amusing, charming
fellow, not very substantial, not very well-
behaved. . . . (All men are the same!)
They bore him no ill-will. . . .

"You see, Annette, if he had been well-
behaved, I wouldn't be here. . . ."

Annette pressed her hand.

"Aie! Don't squeeze so hard!"

After that Sylvie spoke of the florist
shop, where as a child she had sat under
the counter with the fallen flowers and
woven her first dreams,—of her early experiences of Paris life, listening to the talk
of her mother and the customers; then,
when Delphine died (Sylvie had been
thirteen), of her apprenticeship to a dress-

maker, who had been her mother's friend
and who had taken her in; then, after a
year and the death of her employer who
had been worn out by work (one wears out
quickly in Paris!), of her various avatars.
Harsh notations, bitter experiences, always
gaily told, seen with drollery. In passing
she painted types and characters, pricking
with a needle on the weft of her narrative, a trait, a witticism, a word, or a face.
She did not tell all; she had experimented
with life a little more than she admitted,
perhaps more than she cared to remember.
She caught herself up short at the chapter
on her friend,—of her last friend (if there
had been other chapters, she kept them to
herself.) A medical student, met at a ball
in the quartier. (She would willingly go
without dinner, to dance!) Not very handsome, but nice; big and brown, with
laughing eyes that wrinkled at the corners; turned up nostrils, the nose of a good
dog; amusing, affectionate. She described
him with no trimmings, but with complaisance, praising his good qualities, as
well as poking a little fun at him, satisfied

with her choice. She interrupted herself
to laugh at certain memories which she
recounted, and at others which she did not.
Annette, all ears, troubled and interested,
was silent save for a few embarrassed words
that she slipped in here and there. Sylvie
held her hand, and with her other free
hand she caressed the ends of Annette's
fingers, one by one, while she spoke, as
though she were plucking a garland. Per-
ceiving her sister's embarrassment, she loved
her for it and was amused by it.

The two young girls were seated on a
bench beneath the trees, and they could no
longer see each other in the darkness that
had fallen. Sylvie, little devil, profited
by this to describe scenes that were a trifle
indecorous and decidedly amorous, so that
she might completely intimidate her big
sister. Annette sensed her malice, and did
not know whether she should smile or censure; she would have liked to censure, but
her little sister was so pretty! There was
so much laughter in her voice, her joy
seemed so wholesome! Annette scarcely
breathed, trying to hide the tumult into

which these amorous stories threw her.
Sylvie, who could feel beneath her fingers
the other's emotions, paused to enjoy the
situation and to concoct some new deviltry:
leaning towards Annette, she asked her
frankly, in a lowered voice, if she too had
a sweetheart. Annette started—she had
not expected this—and blushed. Sylvie's
piercing eyes sought to see her features in
the protective gloom, and, failing this, she
ran her fingers over Annette's cheek. . . .

"It's on fire," she said, laughing.

Annette laughed awkwardly, and blushed
more furiously. Sylvie flung herself on
her neck.

"My dear little stupid, what a darling
you are! No, you are priceless! Don't
be hurt! I'm mistaken. I love you de-
votedly. Love your Sylvie a little. She's
not much good, but such as she is she's
yours. Annette, my ducky! Hold out
your lips; I love you!"

Passionately Annette clasped her in her
arms, taking her breath away. Sylvie, dis-
engaging herself, observed in the tone of
a connoisseur:

"You know how to kiss all right. Who taught you?"

Annette rudely shut the girl's mouth with her hand.

"Don't be always joking!"

Sylvie kissed her palm.

"Forgive me, I won't do it any more."

And, with her cheek resting on her sister's arm, Sylvie remained discreetly silent, listening, watching against the obscure transparence of a patch of sky, hollowed out of the semi-darkness by the branches of the trees, Annette's face which was bent toward her as she spoke in a low voice.

Annette was opening her heart. In her turn she was telling of the happy plenitude of her solitary youth, that dawn of a little Diana, passionate but untroubled, who took joy in what she desired no less than in what she possessed, for between the one and the other there was for her only the distance between to-day and to-morrow. And she was so sure of the morrow that she tasted in advance the perfume of jasmine on the trellis, without hastening to gather it.

She described the calm egotism of those

years, empty of events but rich in the sweetness of dreams. She told of the intimacy, the absorbing affection, that bound her to her father. And, in telling about herself, she had the singular experience of discovering herself; for, until this moment, she had never had occasion to analyse her past. She was, momentarily, frightened by it. She halted in her narrative; now she had difficulty in expressing herself, now she expressed herself with a troubled, pictorial ardor. Sylvie did not always understand and was amused, but she listened less than she observed the expression of face, voice and body.

Annette now confessed the jealous suffering she had felt at discovery of the second family that her father had hidden from her, and the turmoil into which she had been thrown by the existence of a rival, a sister. With her burning frankness, she dissimulated nothing that had made her blush; her passion reawakened as she evoked it. She said, "I hated you! . . ." in so fierce a tone that she stopped, checked by the sound of her own voice. Sylvie, much less stirred but deeply interested, felt Annette's hand trembling against her cheek, and thought:

"There is fire, underneath there!"

Annette had picked up the thread of the confession that were costing her so dear. And Sylvie was saying to herself:

"How funny she is to tell me all this!"

But she felt growing within her a respect for her strange, big sister; it was mocking, certainly, but infinitely tender, and it made her rub her cheek cajolingly against the sisterly palm. . . .

Annette had come to the point in her narrative at which the attraction of her unknown sister had taken possession of her, despite her resistance, the point at which she had seen Sylvie for the first time. But here frankness could not conquer the emotion of her heart. She tried to go on, stopped, gave it up, and said:

"I can't. . . ."

There was silence. Sylvie was smiling. She stood up, put her face close to her sister's, and, pinching her chin, she whispered very low:

"You are a great lover."

"I!" protested Annette, thoroughly confused.

Sylvie had risen from the bench, and, standing in front of her sister, she pressed Annette's head against her body and said:

"Poor . . . poor Annette! . . ."

VIII

After this, the two sisters saw each other
constantly. Not a week went by without
their getting together. Sylvie would come
to Boulogne in the evening to surprise Annette. More rarely Annette went to Sylvie's. By a tacit agreement they so arranged things that Annette should not
meet the friend. They adopted a regular
day for lunching together at the creamery,
and played at making rendezvous here and
there in Paris. They took an equal pleasure
in being together. It became a necessity.
The hours dragged on the days when they
did not see each other; the old aunt could
not succeed in breaking Annette's silence,
and Sylvie was a sullen puzzle to her sweetheart, who was in no way to blame. The
one thing that made the waiting bearable
was the thought of all that they would
have to say to each other when they met
again. But this consolation did not always
suffice, and never was Annette happier than

on one evening when Sylvie rang her bell, after ten o'clock, saying that she could not wait until the morrow to kiss her. Annette was eager to have her stay with her; but the little one, who had sworn that she had only five minutes to stay, had gone off on the run, like a shot, without a word, after an hour of prattling.

Annette would have liked Sylvie to enjoy the benefit of her house and her worldly goods. But Sylvie had a brusque way of avoiding all temptations; she had got it into her head—her obstinate little head— that she would accept no monetary loan. On the other hand, she made no fuss about accepting a toilet article, or even "borrowing" it (what she borrowed she forgot to return). It even happened that once or twice she snitched . . . oh! nothing important! . . . And, of course, she would never have touched a bit of money. Money, that's sacred! But a little knickknack, a valueless ornament: she couldn't resist it. Annette had noticed this trick of the little *gazza ladra*, and she was embarrassed by it. Why didn't Sylvie ask her? She would

have been so happy to give! She tried not
to see. But the sisters found their greatest
pleasure in exchanging a blouse, a corset
cover, underwear: Annette's love fed on
this. Sylvie was an expert in the art of
fixing her sister's dresses, and her taste
modified Annette's more sober taste. The
effect was not always very happy, for Annette in her excess of enthusiasm would
sometimes exaggerate the imitation beyond
what suited her individual style, and Sylvie,
amused, would have to restrain her zeal.
Much more cautious, she knew how, without admitting it, to profit by what she
learned from Annette's sober distinction,—
certain shades of speech, gesture and manner; but her copy was so cunning that one
would have thought that her model had
borrowed from her.

Yet, despite their intimacy, Annette succeeded in becoming familiar with only a
part of her sister's life. Sylvie enjoyed her
independence, and she liked to make it felt.
At bottom she had never completely dis-
armed herself of her class hostility; An-

nette saw clearly that she was determined
to have no one run her affairs or enter
into her life save when she pleased. Besides, Sylvie's self-love had not failed to
observe that her sister did not approve of
everything about her. Notably her love
affair. Although Annette tried to accept it,
she did not know how to dissimulate the
embarrassment that this subject caused her.
Either she fled from it, or, when she was
compelled to speak of it, with the sincere
desire of pleasing Sylvie, there was a forced
note in her tone that Sylvie detected; and
she, with a word, would change the subject. This made Annette sad. With all
her heart she wanted Sylvie to be happy,
happy in her own way. And she did not
wish to show that this way was not the one
she would have preferred. But she did
show it, indubitably. When one's feelings
are strong, one is not very adroit. Sylvie
was hurt by this, and she took revenge in
silence. It was only by chance that Annette learned, several weeks after their oc-
currence, of certain important events in her
young sister's life.

As a matter of fact it was impossible to make Sylvie acknowledge their importance; and, indeed, her elastic temperament may have thrown them off easily, but it was possible, too, that her pride made her pretend that this was so more than was really the case. It was incidentally that Annette learned that "for some time" (impossible to be precise: it was "ancient history") the friend had not been on the scene, the liaison had been broken. Sylvie did not seem at all affected by this; Annette was much more so, but it was not with regret. Awkwardly she tried to find out what had happened. Sylvie shrugged her shoulders, laughed and said:

"Nothing happened. It's happened, that's all."

Annette should have rejoiced, but these words of her sister hurt her. . . . What a strange feeling! How wrong she was! . . . Oh! that word "happen" . . . in the world of the heart! And she could laugh as she said it! . . .

But this great news (it was great news for Annette) was followed shortly by another discovery. One day when Annette announced her intention of coming to meet her sister when the shop let out, Sylvie remarked calmly:

"No, no, I'm not there any more. . . ."

"What?" exclaimed Annette in astonishment. "Since when?"

"Oh, quite a while. . . ."

(Still the same trick of avoiding an exact accounting! It might as well have been last evening as last year!)

"What happened?"

"The same thing that happens every year (just as in *Malbrough* . . . "*sà Paques ou à la Trinité* . . .""): The dead season comes immediately after the Grand-Prix. The employers all back the wrong horse, so as to have a generous excuse for giving us the gate."

"But where are you then?"

"Oh, I'm here and there. I run about and do a little bit of everything."

Annette was in consternation.

"Then you haven't any job, and you didn't tell me!"

With a little air of superiority, Sylvie

explained (at heart not at all displeased by the emotion she had produced) that she slapped together cheap costumes for others to finish, hemmed little dresses, and sewed up men's trousers. And she made a great joke of it all in the telling. But Annette did not laugh. Pressing her inquiry further, she found that her sister was at her wits' end to find work and that she sometimes accepted tasks that were overtiring and disheartening. Now she understood why Sylvie had seemed pale "for some time"; why she had not come to see her for a number of days, offering feeble excuses and absurd lies, in order, no doubt, to spend a part of the night wearing out her fingers and her eyes in sewing. Sylvie, in her joking tone of affected indifference, continued to recount her little misadventures. But she saw that her sister's lips were trembling with anger. And, abruptly, Annette burst out:

"No! It's shameful! I can't, I simply can't bear it! What! you say you love me, and you yourself wanted us to be friends, you pretend to be one, and then you hide from me the most serious things that concern you! . . ."

Sylvie's curled lip said, "Pshaw! What of it! . . ." But Annette did not let her speak; the torrent was loosed.

"I had confidence in you, I thought that you would tell me about your trials and troubles as I tell you about mine, that we would share everything. And then you push me to one side as though I were a stranger; I know nothing, nothing! Except by chance, I should never have learned that you were in trouble, that you are hunting a job, that you are ruining your health; and you would take on any sort of work rather than tell me about it, when you know that it would be a joy for me to help you. . . . It's wrong, wrong! You have hurt me. It's a lack of frankness, a lack of friendship! But I won't stand it any longer! No! . . . To begin with you are coming to live with me, and you are going to stay here until the dead season is over. . . ."

Sylvie shook her head.

"You are coming, don't say no! Now

listen to me, Sylvie; I won't forgive if you don't. If you say no, I will never see you again, in all my life. . . ."

Without taking the trouble to excuse herself or to explain, Sylvie, smiling and obstinate, answered:

"No, my dear, no."

She was quite pleased at Annette's agitation. Her big sister, who had tried to defeat her, was now no longer mistress of herself, she was almost in tears. Sylvie was thinking: "How much prettier she is when she is animated!"

Her face purple with anger, Annette kept repeating, beseeching imperiously:

"Stay! . . . You will stay. . . . I want you to. . . . It's agreed? . . . You are going to stay? . . . You're staying? . . . Answer me! . . . It's yes? . . ."

And with the same exasperating smile, the little donkey replied:

"It's no, dearest."

Annette turned away from her, violently.

"Then, it's all over."

And turning her back, she went to the window, ·where she seemed oblivious to

Sylvie's presence. The younger girl waited for a moment, then she got up and said in a wheedling voice:

"So long, Annette."

Annette did not turn around.

"Farewell," she replied.

Her hands were clenched. If she had moved, Heaven knows what would have happened! She would have wept, cried out. . . . She did not stir, haughty and icy. Sylvie, somewhat embarrassed, and not a little disturbed, but amused in spite of everything, took her departure; once behind the door, she thumbed her nose.

She was not very proud—but a little proud, just the same—of her fine resistance. No more was Annette proud of her rage. In consternation she told herself now that she had burned her bridges: instead of conquering Sylvie by tact and patience, she had practically driven her away. Sylvie would never come back, that was a certainty. Annette, in her dilemma, had closed the door in her sister's face. And she had forbidden herself to reopen it to her. After all her declarations, she could

not go after Sylvie! It would be a confession of defeat. Her pride wouldn't permit it; no more would her sense of justice.
For Sylvie had behaved badly. . . . No,
no, she would not go! . . .

She put on her hat and went straight to
Sylvie's.

Sylvie had returned home. Thought-
fully she was examining the perplexing
situation. She found it stupid, but she
saw no way out; for she did not dream of
bending to Annette's will, and no more
could she believe that Annette would yield.
At bottom she did not think the Duckling
was wrong. But she did not wish to give
in. Sylvie was not insensible to the bless-
ings of fortune. Without its being apparent, Annette's wealth had awakened in
her quite a little temptation and envy.
(One can't help it, even when one is not—
almost not—envious! When one has a
young body, filled with fine little desires,
can one help thinking what one would do
with wealth, and how much better one
would know how to enjoy it than the stupid
people who have had it thrust into their

mouths, all nicely cooked! . . .) She did not admit it to herself, but she begrudged Annette her fortune, a little. Yet, if it was any fault of hers, Annette was trying to win forgiveness for it. But the point was that Sylvie would not pardon her. Oh! no one confesses these things to himself. Every one cherishes in his breast, well hidden, five or six little monsters. One does not boast of them, one seems not to see them; but one is in no hurry at all to get rid of them. . . . A more easily confessed feeling was that Sylvie, tempted by gifts that were denied her, liked to enjoy the luxury of appearing to disdain them. But, as a matter of fact, this luxury was devoid of charm; and it proved of scant service. No, it was decidedly true that Sylvie took no very keen pleasure in her victory. There was nothing to strut about; if she had won, it was at her own cost. What made this conclusion the more painful was that her situation was, in reality, decidedly unpleasant; and Sylvie was having a deal of difficulty in extricating her-

self from the scrape. The number of girls
out of work was considerable, and naturally
the employers took advantage of the situation. Nor was her health so splendid.
The crushing heat of a torrid July, late
hours, poor food, and bad drinking water
had brought on an attack of enteritis which
had left her in a weakened condition.
Under the gridiron of her roof that was
roasted by the sun, with blinds closed,
Sylvie, half undressed, with burning skin,
seeking some cool thing on which to lay
her hands, was thinking how comfortable
it would be in the Boulogne house; and as
she was abundantly endowed with irony, in
default of other gifts, she was making fun
of her own stupidity. She had done well!
. . . And to think that she and Annette
were in accord, at bottom! Now they were
at logger-heads. Good Heavens! how
stupid they were! Neither one would give
in! . . .

And being perfectly sure that she would
not yield, that she would be stupid to the
last, she was smiling, curling her pale lips,

when she heard Annette's impetuous steps in the hall. She recognized them immediately, and bounded to her feet.

"Annette was coming back! . . . The darling girl! . . ."

She hadn't waited for her. . . . Annette was certainly "the best ever! . . ."

Annette was already in the room. Flushed with excitement and with the heat of her journey, she had no idea what she was going to do; but the moment she entered she knew immediately. Suffocated by the furnace-like atmosphere which pervaded the half-darkened room, she was again seized by a passionate anger. She marched up to Sylvie, who flung herself on her neck; she seized the girl's damp shoulders in impatient hands, and, without responding to her kisses, she said in an exasperated voice:

"I'm taking you away. . . . Get dressed! And don't argue!"

Sylvie argued just the same, in order not to lose the habit. She made a protesting face. But she surrendered herself. Annette imperiously dressed her, put on her shoes, buttoned her blouse, abruptly clapped her hat on her head, shoved her about like a parcel. Sylvie kept saying, "No, no, no," uttering indignant little cries for form's sake; but she was delighted at being bullied. When Annette had finished, Sylvie seized both her hands and kissed them, leaving the mark of her teeth upon them; then, laughing happily, she said:

"There's nothing else to do. . . . Madame Tempest! I surrender. . . . Carry me off!"

Annette carried her off. She had taken the girl's arm in her strong hands, that gripped like a vise. They got into a taxi. When they arrived, Sylvie said to Annette:

"Now I can tell you: well . . . I was dying to come."

"Why were you so bad?" demanded Annette, grumbling and happy.

Sylvie took Annette's hand, and with the curved index finger she tapped her own round little forehead.

"Yes, there's mischief in there!" exclaimed Annette.

"Just like yours," said Sylvie, showing her their two obstinate foreheads in the mirror. They were smiling at each other.

"And," added Sylvie, "we know whom that comes from."

IX

Sylvie's room had been awaiting her for a long time. Even before knowing of Sylvie's existence, Annette had kept the cage ready for the friend who would come. The friend had not come; barely had her shadow been glimpsed, on two or three occasions. Annette's personality, which was sufficiently individual, her manners, alternately chilly and ardent, the impetuous character of the outbursts that overcame a reserved nature; and a certain quality that was strange, exigent and imperious, which, without her suspecting it, showed in flashes, even when she was permeated by the desire to give herself with a passionate humility, —all these things frightened away the young girls of her own age, who without doubt esteemed her and appreciated her essence (so to speak), but prudently and from a distance. Sylvie was the first to take possession of the friendly cage. One may be certain that she did not worry about

95

it, and that it would not disturb her to
leave it when the day came that she so
pleased. She was not much intimidated by
Annette. She did not even feel any surprise at the room in which she was installed. On her first visit, from certain
little marks of ingenious affection, and
from Annette's awkward confusion in
showing it to her, she had guessed that it
must be meant for her.

Now that she admitted her defeat—to
her own gain—she no longer offered the
least resistance. Still languid from her
attack of enteritis, the little convalescent
abandoned herself to the coddling with
which her sister surrounded her. The
doctor who was called in had found her
anemic, and had recommended a change
of air, a visit to the mountains. But
neither of the girls was in a hurry to leave
the common nest; and, cajolers that they
were, they knew how to make the doctor
say that, after all, Boulogne was well
enough, and even, in a sense, that it was
better for Sylvie first to regain her strength

by a complete rest, before seeking the tonic
of keen mountain air.

So Sylvie could indulge herself, and idle
in bed. It was so long since she had been
able to do that! It was delicious to sleep
her fill, to make up for all the sleeps that
she had lost, and—most delicious of all—
to rest without sleeping, her limbs stretched
out between the fine, soft sheets, her body
experiencing the ultimate in drowsiness and
happiness, while she searched with her foot
for cool corners in the bed. And to dream,
to dream! . . . Oh! they didn't go far,
those dreams! Like a fly on the ceiling,
they turned round and round. They did
not even come to the end of a phrase.
Twenty times, with sticky tongue, they repeated a story, a project, a memory of the
shop, of love, or of a hat. In the midst
of it they jumped head first again into the
pool of sleep. . . .

"But see here, Sylvie, see here . . ."
(she would protest dreamily), "That's no
life. . . . Please get out of it!"

Half opening one eye, she would see her

sister leaning over her, and she would make an effort (the words barely came out) to say:

"Annette!   Wake me up."

Annette would say, "Little rascal!" and laugh, shaking her. Sylvie would play the baby.

"Oh, dear mamma, what have I done to be so sleepy?"

Annette's great love overflowed in maternal transports. Seated on the bed, it seemed to her that the dear head which she pressed against her breast was that of her daughter. Sylvie surrendered, with little plaintive protests:

"But how shall I ever be able to go back to work, afterwards?"

"You shan't work any more."

"Why, yes, I will, the idea!" Sylvie rebelled.

In an instant she was awake; pulling herself away from her sister, sitting up straight, the tousled girl fixed Annette with a look that defied her.

"So she still thinks that we want to keep her here by force! Get along with you,

my girl!" said Annette, laughing. "Go, if
your heart tells you to! No one is keep-
ing you."

"If that's the case, I'll stay!" exclaimed
the spirit of contradiction. And Sylvie
slipped down into the bed again, tired from
her effort.

But this indolence lasted for only a few
days; and after that, when she was satiated
with sleep, there came the time when it
was impossible to keep her quiet. She
traipsed about all day long, half dressed:
in her sister's slippers that were too big
for her bare feet, in her sister's peignor
that she tucked up toga fashion, with bare
arms and legs, she went from room to room,
looking at everything, exploring everything.
She had not much notion of "thine."
("Mine" was another matter!) Annette
having said to her, "You are at home," she
had taken her at her word. She rummaged
everywhere. She tried everything. She
splashed for hours in the bath room. There
was not a corner that she left uninspected.
Annette found Sylvie with her nose in her
papers, but these had bored her very

quickly. And the amazed aunt received the invasion of the little half-dressed figure who ferreted about amongst all the furniture, moved everything around, addressed a few pretty words to their owner (who was following her every movement in fear and trembling) and then left everything in disorder, and the old lady at once scandalized and charmed.

The house was filled with an inexhaustible babble, with a chattering that had neither head nor tail, no end, and no reason to end. In no matter what place, in no matter what costume, perched on the arm of an easy chair, or comb in hand arranging their hair, or abruptly halted upon a step of the stairs, or in bathrobes after the morning tub,— the two friends talked, talked, talked; and, once started, this might last for hours or days. They forgot to go to bed; their aunt protested in vain, coughed, rapped on the ceiling. They tried to put a mute on their voices, to stifle their laughter; but at the end of five minutes . . . Pouf! Sylvie's little hautboys began to shrill, and there sounded the happy or indignant exclama-

tions of Annette, who was always getting
into a tangle, and whom the younger girl
could easily put up a tree. This time the
raps on the ceiling became really annoyed.
Then they decided to "hit the hay"; but
they still kept it up while they undressed.
The two rooms adjoined, the doors were
left open, and they were constantly crossing their frontiers, talking in skirts, talking without skirts; and they would have
talked all night long, from one bed to the
other, had not the sleep of youth come suddenly to put an end to their cluckling. It
swooped down upon them in a flash, as a
sparrow-hawk upon a chicken. They fell
back upon their pillows, with open mouths,
in the middle of a phrase. Annette slept
like a lump; her sleep was heavy, frequently disturbed, stormy, drenched with
dreams; she rumpled the sheets, she talked
in her sleep, but she never awakened.
Sylvie, a light sleeper with a tiny snore (if
you had told her that, she would have
cloaked herself in wounded dignity), would
awake and listen in amusement to her sister's gibberish; sometimes she would get

up and go over to the bed where Annette
lay prostrate, with the sheets thrust up in
a mountain by her crossed knees; and,
bending over in the light of the night-lamp
(for Annette could not sleep without a
light), Sylvie would fascinatedly watch the
dull, heavy but strangely passionate, sometimes tragic face of the sleeper who was
drowning in the ocean of her dreams. She
no longer recognized her. . . .

"Annette? That? That's my sister? . . ."

She wanted to waken her abruptly and
put her arms about her neck.

"Wolf, are you there?"

But she was too sure that the wolf was.
there to try the experiment. Less pure
and more normal than her dangerous elder
sister, she played with fire, but she was not
burned by it.

They studied each other at length, while
they were dressing and undressing, com-
paring themselves curiously. Annette had
fits of primitive modesty that amused Sylvie, who was at once freer and franker.
Annette often appeared cold, one would

have said almost hostile; she went into
tantrums, or she wept without cause. The
fine Lyonnaise poise, of which she had formerly been so proud, seemed definitely lost.
And the worst of it was—that she did not
at all regret it.

Their confidences went further, now. It
would not be easy to reproduce them all.
It comes quite naturally to young girls who
love each other to calmly say audacious
things in their conversation, things that in
their mouths preserve a semi-innocence, but
which would have none were they repeated
by another. In these talks the difference
of their two natures was clearly shown: the
laughing, child-like, perfectly assured un-
morality of the one; and the passionate,
disquieting, electrically charged seriousness
of the other. There were clashes; Annette
was exasperated by the greedy levity and
wilful bawdiness with which Sylvie discussed amorous subjects. Audacious in her
soul, she was reserved in her words; it
seemed that she feared to hear what she
thought. She had fits of shutting herself
up in a double tower, in a fierce dumbness

that she herself did not quite understand. Sylvie understood it much better. After she had lived with her for fifteen days, Sylvie knew Annette better than Annette knew herself.

Yet it was not that her mental faculties lifted her above the average of an agreeable Paris working girl. Aside from a practical sense that was very sound and cautious—but from which she never drew the most possible profit, because she almost always preferred to obey her caprices—she did not emerge from her own sphere to any great extent. Certainly everything amused her, but nothing really interested her except fashions. As for everything that had to do with art—pictures, music, books—she never got beyond the most ordinary stage of appreciation, and sometimes she didn't reach that. Annette was often embarrassed by her taste. Sylvie would realize it, and say:

"Ouf! I've put my foot in it again. . . . Well, tell me someone who behaves properly in society! . . ."

(She spoke of a picture as one speaks of a hat.)

"What should one admire? Once I know, I shall be able to do it as well as anyone else. . . ."

But on other occasions she was not so conciliatory; she held out stoutly for the hero of some newspaper serial or for some insipid romance which was to her the last word in art and sentiment. However, she obliged her elder sister to discover the value, or rather the artistic promise, of a genre that Annette had always insisted on running down without knowing anything about it: the movies, which Sylvie adored, indiscriminately.

It sometimes happened, too, that although she was incapable of feeling the beauty of a book which they were reading together, Sylvie understood better than Annette the power of certain pages, whose strange truth disconcerted her sister; for Sylvie knew life better than Annette did. And that is the Book of Books. Read it not who will. Everyone carries it in himself, written

from the first to the last line. But to de-
cipher it, one must be taught the language
by the harsh master Experience. Sylvie
had received lessons from him at an early
age; she read fluently. Annette was beginning late. Slower to reach her, the lessons
were to sink deeper.

X

The summer, this year, was excessively hot. By the middle of August the beautiful trees in the garden were already parched. In the close nights, Sylvie gasped for a passing breath of air. She had recuperated, but she was still wan and had little appetite. She was always a small eater, and if she could have had her way she would have frequently dined on nothing but an ice and fruit. But Annette kept watch over her, Annette grumbled. She was kept busy. Finally she decided on the trip to the mountains, that had been put off from week to week with the underlying hope that it might be avoided. She would have liked to keep her sister entirely to herself, all summer long.

They repaired to a spot in the Grisons that Annette remembered from a former visit as having a good, simple hotel, in a pastoral, restful setting of old Switzerland. But a few years had transformed everything. The hotel was swarming with people. It was a city of pretentious palaces. Automobile roads cut through the fields; and, in the depths of the woods, one could hear the grinding of an electric tramway. Annette wished to flee. But they were tired from a night and day of suffocating travel; they did not know where to go, and all they asked was to lie stretched out without stirring. Where they were, even if everything else had changed, the air at least had preserved its crystalline purity; Sylvie sucked it in with her tongue, as though she were licking a Parisian ice from a glass cup while she stood beside the cart of an ambulatory merchant in the midst of a roaring street. They told themselves they would stay for a few days, until it became a little cooler. And then they got used to it. They discovered the charm of the place.

It was a lively season. A tennis tournament was attracting the alert youth of three or four nations. There were informal dances, little plays. A buzzing swarm was loafing, flirting, showing off. Annette could have done without it; but Sylvie was frankly entertained, and the pleasure that she showed communicated itself to her sister. Both were high-spirited and had no reason to frown on the diversions of their age.

Young, gay and attractive, each in her own way, it was not long before they were very much surrounded. Annette was blooming. In the open air and at sports she showed to her best advantage. Strong, strapping, fond of walking and all active games, she was a brilliant tennis partner, with a sure eye, supple wrist, quick hand, and lightning-like return. Usually restrained in her gestures, she displayed, when occasion demanded, admirable nerve and furious bursts of speed. Sylvie, marvelling, clapped her hands as she watched her leap about; she was proud of her sister. She admired her the more because she felt incapable of imitating her: this svelte Parisienne was inept at all sports, and she did not particularly understand their attraction. They called for too much action! She found it more agreeable—and above

all, more prudent—to remain a spectator.
But she did not waste her time. . . .

She formed a little court, over which
she queened it as though she had done
nothing else all her life. Sly one that she
was, she knew how to copy from the fash-
ionable young women she observed all those
mannerisms that were well-bred, smart,
and easily borrowed. Looking as though
butter would not melt in her mouth, deli-
ciously distrait, her eyes and ears were always open; she missed nothing. But Annette still remained her best model. With
a sure instinct, she knew not only how to
copy her in many a detail, but how to improve the copy by slight changes, and even
in certain cases how to take the opposite
tack,—oh! just enough to appear incor-
rect, by one refinement the more. She
showed still more intelligence by never
overstepping the limits within which she
felt solid ground beneath her feet. In her
own province she was perfect, in manners,
bearing, and tone. Exquisite distinction
raised to an extravagant point. Annette
could not help laughing when she heard

Sylvie, with charming aplomb, retailing to
her court little tid-bits with which Annette
had stuffed her the evening before. Sylvie
would slip her a sly wink. It would not
have done, certainly, to push her too far
in conversation. For all her wit and excellent memory, she would have gotten her
foot into it; but she didn't slip, she watched
her step. And then, too, she knew how to
choose her partners. The majority of them
were young sportsmen from foreign lands:
Anglo-Saxons, Roumanians, who were more
sensitive to a mistake in play than to an
error in language. The great favorite of
the little feminine circle was an Italian.
Bearing the sonorous name of an old Lom-
bard family (extinct for centuries, but the
name never dies), he was of a type that is
very common among the youth of the
Peninsula, and which is characteristic of a
period rather than of a race. In it one
finds curiously blended the American of
Fifth Avenue, and the condottiere of the
fourteenth century, which gives to the
ensemble a rather grand air—(Operatic).
A handsome fellow, tall and straight, well

built, with a round head and clean shaven
face, very brown skin, fiery eyes, a great
conquering nose, bluish nostrils, and a heavy
jaw, Tullio walked with supple loins and
chest thrust out. His manners were a mixture of hauteur, obsequious courtesy, and
brutality. An irresistible man. He had
but to stoop to gather hearts. He did not
stoop. He waited for them to be placed
in his hand.

Perhaps it was precisely for the reason
that Annette did not offer hers to him that
he first fixed his choice on her. A tennis
champion himself, he appreciated the physical qualities of the robust girl, and when
he talked with her he discovered other
sports for which they had a common liking:
horseback riding and canoeing, which Annette had gone into with the passion that
she brought to everything. With his big
nose he sensed the over-abundant energy
that coursed through her virgin body; and
he desired it. Annette perceived this desire, and she was at once offended and cap-
tivated. Her intense physical life, which
had been curbed by years of semi-claustra-

tion, was awakening under the flame of this superb summer, in the midst of these young people who thought only of pleasure, and in the excitement of these vigorous sports. The last weeks spent with Sylvie, their free conversations, and the excessive affection with which she was saturated, had considerably perturbed her nature,—that nature which she so little understood, unsuspecting its depths. The house was ill defended against an assault of the senses. For the first time, Annette experienced the sting of sexual passion. It caused her shame and anger, as though someone had slapped her face. But this did not make the desire wane. Instead of hiding herself, she faced the onslaught with a cold pride and a trembling heart. As for Tullio, who always cloaked a rapacious desire beneath a perfect deference, he was the more enamoured when he saw that she understood and was ready to oppose him. This was another match, differently passionate! Harsh challenges were exchanged, there were sharp passages at arms, without any sign of these things on the surface. As he bowed with masculine politeness to kiss her hand, while she was smiling at him with a haughty grace, she read in his eyes:

"I shall have you."

And her shut lips answered him:

"Never!"

Sylvie was following the duel with the eyes of a lynx; and while she found it amusing, she felt that she would like to play a part in it. What part? Really, she had no idea on that point. . . . Well, to amuse herself, and to second Annette of course, that went without saying! The boy was good-looking; Annette was good-looking too. How beautifying a strong feeling always is! That burning pride, that little bull's forehead ready for combat, those waves of red and white that Sylvie imagined she could see passing over Annette's body, like shivers. . . . The man was priding himself on his play. . . .

". . . Nothing to be done, my lad; no, no, you won't get her if she doesn't want you to! But does she want it? Doesn't she want it? Make up your mind, Annette! He's caught. Finish him off! . . .

The stupid! She doesn't know. . . . All right, we're going to help her. . . ."

Their acquaintance was founded on praises of Annette. They both admired her. The Italian was definitely conquered. Radiant, with her eyes shining, Sylvie was entirely of his opinion. She was very adroit in her praising of Annette; but she was no less so in arming herself with all her charms. And once she had brought them into play, there was no way of stopping them. In vain she would say to them:

"Now, be quiet. That's enough. You are going too far. . . ."

But her charms no longer listened, there was nothing to do but to let them have their way. . . . And it was so amusing! Naturally, that idiot had taken fire immediately. How silly men are! He thought that if anyone was nice to him, it must be for his beauty. . . . But he was handsome, just the same. . . . And now what would the fish do, between two hooks? Was he going to presume to gobble them both? What was he going to decide? . . . "Well, old chap, make a choice!"

She did not facilitate his choice for him by effacing herself in favor of Annette. And no more did Annette. From now on she instinctively redoubled her efforts in order to eclipse Sylvie. The two sisters were devoted to each other. Sylvie was as proud of the praise given Annette as Annette was of the impression produced by Sylvie. They took counsel together; each supervised the details of the other's toilet. With an unerring sense, they knew how to serve as a foil to each other. At the evening parties in the hotel they attracted all eyes. But, in spite of themselves, they came to be looked upon as rivals. And when they danced, neither one could help evaluating the success of the other, no matter how severely both forbade themselves to do this. Especially success with the man who was, decidedly, preoccupying them much more than they would have wished. . . . And he preoccupied them the more now that he was uncertain which of them preoccupied him the more. Annette began to feel vaguely miserable when she saw Tullio in ardent attendance upon her sister.

Both girls were good dancers, each in her
own manner. Annette did all that she
could to establish her superiority; and it
was certain that she danced better in the
eyes of the connoisseurs. But Sylvie, while
less correct, had more abandon; and as soon
as she realized Annette's intention she became irresistible. Nor did Tullio resist.
To Annette came the sorrow of seeing herself forsaken. After a succession of dances
with Sylvie, Tullio and she went out together, talking and laughing, into the fine
summer night. Annette could no longer
control herself. She too had to quit the
room. Without daring to follow them into
the garden, she tried to catch sight of them
from the glassed-in gallery that led into
the garden; and she did see them, on the
path,—she saw them bending towards each
other, exchanging kisses as they walked.

But the pain of this was nothing to what
followed. When Annette, sitting in the
dark after having gone up to her room,
saw Sylvie come in, all animation, and
when Sylvie exclaimed at finding her alone
in the darkness, kissed her cheek, and

showed a thousand and one signs of usual affection; when Annette, after giving the excuse of a sudden headache that had obliged her to retire, asked Sylvie how she had spent the rest of the evening and if she had gone walking with Tullio, Sylvie ingenuously replied that she had not gone walking and that she did not know what had become of Tullio; that besides Tullio was beginning to bore her, and then she didn't like men who were too handsome, and besides he was foppish, and he was a little too dark. . . . Upon which she went to bed, humming a waltz.

Annette did not sleep. Sylvie slept soundly; she had no suspicion of the tempest she had unchained. . . . Annette was the prey of unleashed demons. What had happened was a catastrophe, a double catastrophe. Sylvie was her rival, and Sylvie was lying to her. Sylvie, her beloved! Sylvie, her joy and her faith! . . . Everything was crumbling. She could no longer love her. No longer love her? Could she, could she no longer love her? . . . Oh, how deep-rooted that love was, so much

more so than she had thought! . . . But
is it possible to love someone whom one dis-
trusts?   Oh!   Sylvie's treachery wouldn't
be anything. . . . There was something
else. It was. . . . It was. . . . Go ahead,
say what it was! . . . Yes, it was that man,
whom Annette did not respect, whom she
did not love, and whom she loved now.
. . . Loved? No! . . . Whom she *wanted*.
A fever of jealous pride demanded that
she take him, that she tear him away from
the *other;* and, above all, that the other
should not tear him away from her. . . .
("*The other*," that was what Sylvie had
become for Annette! . . .)

That night she did not rest a single hour.
The sheets burned her skin. And from the
neighboring bed there rose the light breathing of the sleep of innocence.

When they found themselves face to face
the next morning, Sylvie saw at a glance
that everything had changed; and she did
not understand what had happened. Annette, with circles under her eyes, pale,
hard and haughty, but strangely more beautiful (at once more beautiful and more

homely, as though all her secret forces had arisen in answer to a summons)—Annette, helmeted in pride, cold, hostile, with a wall about her, looked at Sylvie and listened while she chattered as usual, then scarcely said good-morning, and left the room. . . . Sylvie's babble stopped in the middle of a word. She too went out, and with her eyes followed Annette who was descending the stairs. . . .

She understood. Annette had caught sight of Tullio, who was seated in the hall, and crossing the room she went straight to him. He too recognized that the situation had changed. She sat down beside him. They talked banalities. With her head up, disdainful, she stared straight ahead, avoiding looking at him. But he had no doubt: it was he she was staring at. Under her bluish eyelids, that glance, which she was hiding as though to avoid a too intense light, was saying:

"Do you want me?"

And he, relating an insipid story in a satisfied tone, while he contemplated his

finger nails,—he, like a big cat, was peering sidelong at that body with its firm
breasts, and asking:

"So you want it too?"

"I want you to want me," was the reply.

Sylvie did not hesitate. Making a turn
of the hall, she came and took a chair between Annette and Tullio. Annette's irritation was betrayed in a glance, in only
one: that was enough. Sylvie received its
contempt full in the face. She blinked
her eyelids and pretended not to see, but
she bristled like a cat that has felt an electric current; she smiled, and held herself
ready to bite. The three-handed, fair-
spoken duel began. Annette, ignoring Sylvie's presence, taking no notice of what she
said, talked over her head to Tullio, who
was embarrassed; or, when she was compelled to listen—for the other had a glib
tongue—she called attention with a smile
or an ironic word to one of those minute
grammatical errors that still adorned Sylvie's discourse (for, despite her skill, the
little gossip had not succeeded in weeding

them all from her garden). Sylvie, mortally wounded, no longer saw her sister, she saw only a rival, and she thought:

"You'll get yours."

And, showing her teeth:

"A tooth for a tooth, and an eye for an eye. . . . No, both eyes for one. . . ."

And she threw herself into the fray. Imprudent Annette! Sylvie was not hampered, as she was, by her pride: any weapon was good enough for her, so long as she won. Annette, armored in pride, would have thought herself degraded had she allowed Tullio to glimpse a shadow of her desires. Sylvie was embarrassed by no such scruples; she was going to play with the gentleman the game that flattered him most. . . .

"Which do you prefer? Do you like to inspire a fine disdain, or admiration? . . ."

She knew man: the vain animal. Tullio adored incense, and she gave him full measure. With a calm, ingenuous impudence the little rogue listed the perfections of the young Gattamelata of the Palace Hotel: body, mind, and clothing. Clothing

principally, for she was right in thinking
that this was his chief pride. All homage
pleased him. To be sure. But that he was
handsome was no credit to him; and as regarded his mind, his great name was a
guarantee of that. But his dress was his
individual work, and he was susceptible to
the approbation of an expert Parisienne.
With the eye of a connoisseur, secretly
amused at certain glaring naïvetés of taste,
Sylvie admired everything from top to bottom. Annette blushed from shame and
anger; her small sister's ruse seemed so
crude to her that she asked herself: "Can
he possibly bear it?"

He bore it very well: Tullio was lapping
up milk. When she had descended, step
by step, from the orange cravat to the lilac
belt, to the shoes of green and gold, Sylvie
suddenly stopped: she had an idea. While
going into raptures over the delicacy of
Tullio's feet (he was very proud of them),
she exhibited her own, which were decidedly pretty. With a roguish coquetry
she put them next to Tullio's, she compared
them, showing her leg up to the knee.

Then, turning to Annette, who was disdain-
fully leaning back in her rocking chair, she
said with a delicious smile:

"Let's see yours too, dear!"

And with a rapid gesture she uncovered
them, along with Annette's thick ankles and
the rather heavy columns of her legs. For
two seconds only. Annette clutched at the
malicious little claw, and it withdrew, contented. Tullio had seen. . . .

Nor did she stop there. All morning
long she brought about apparently unpre-
meditated comparisons from which Annette did not emerge to advantage. Under
pretext of appealing to Tullio's superior
taste regarding a collar, a blouse, or a scarf,
she managed to draw attention to what was
certainly not her worst feature, and not
Annette's best. Annette, boiling within,
pretending not to understand, had to hold
herself back to keep from strangling her.
Between two of her tricks, Sylvie, ever
charming, would press her fingers to her
mouth and throw Annette a kiss. But
there were times when their flashing eyes
clashed. . . .

(Annette)—"I loathe you!"

(Sylvie)—"Possibly.   But it's me he loves."

"No, no!" Annette would cry.

"Yes, yes!" retorted Sylvie.

They exchanged challenging glances.

But Annette was not strong enough to hide her animosity for long beneath a smile, like that little snake beneath the flowers. Had she remained, she would have screamed.   Abruptly she left the field free to Sylvie.   She went off with her head high, flinging a last look of defiance at her sister.   And Sylvie's mocking eyes replied:

"Who laughs last, laughs best."

XI

The battle continued the next day, and the days following, beneath the eyes of an amused gallery; for the people in the hotel had seen how things stood; twenty pairs of idle eyes were watching, bets were made. The two rivals were too much preoccupied with their own game to give a thought to that of the others.

The truth was that, for them, it was a game no longer. Sylvie, as well as Annette, was seriously involved. A demon troubled them, goading their senses. Tullio, proud of his victory, had no trouble adding fuel to the flame. He was really handsome, he did not lack wit, he burned with the desires that he had fired: he was worth conquering. None knew it better than he.

Every evening the two hostile sisters met in their rooms. They hated each other; yet they pretended not to know it. Bed neighbors at night, their position would have become untenable had they admitted the fact to themselves; it would have come to a public rupture, a thing they wished to avoid. They so arranged it that they came and went at different times, talked no longer, pretended not to see each other; or, as that was practically impossible, they would coldly say, "Good-morning," and "Good-evening," as though nothing were the matter. The most straightforward, sensible thing would have been to come to an understanding. But they did not wish to. They could not. When passion is unleashed in a woman there is no longer any question of straightforwardness, still less of common sense.

In Annette passion had become a poison. A kiss that Tullio, profiting by his strength, had violently imprinted upon the mouth of the proud girl, one evening at a turn in the path, had unchained in her a sensual torrent. Humiliated and enraged, she fought against it. But she was the less capable of resistance because it was the first time the flood had invaded her. Misfortune of too well defended hearts! When passion

enters, the chastest is the most abandoned. . . .

One night, in one of those fits of feverish
insomnia that were consuming her, Annette
slipped into sleep while thinking she was
still awake. She saw herself lying on her
bed, with open eyes; but she could not
budge, her limbs were bound. She knew
that Sylvie, at her side, was pretending to
sleep, and that Tullio was going to come.
She could already hear the floor creak in
the corridor, and the shuffle of cautious
steps advancing. She saw Sylvie raise herself from the pillow, swing her legs from
under the sheets, get up, and slip towards
the door that half opened. Annette wanted
to get up too, but she could not. As
though she had heard her, Sylvie turned
around, came back to the bed, looked at
her, leaned over to see her better. She
was not at all, not at all, like Sylvie: she
did not resemble her, and yet it was
Sylvie; she laughed wickedly, uncovering
her teeth; she had long black hair, straight
and stiff, that fell over her face when she

leaned down, and brushed Annette's mouth and eyes. Annette felt on her tongue the taste of a rough mane and its hot odor. The face of her rival came closer, closer. Sylvie opened the bed, and got into it. Annette felt a hard knee pressing against her hip. She was suffocating. Sylvie had a knife; the chill blade grazed Annette's throat, and she struggled, screamed. . . . She found herself in the quiet of her room, sitting up in bed, the sheets in confusion. Sylvie was sleeping peaceably. Annette, quelling the beating of her heart, listened to her sister's reassuring breathing; and still she trembled from hate and horror. . . .

She hated. . . . But whom? . . . And who was it that she loved? She appraised Tullio, she did not respect him, she mistrusted him, she had no confidence in him whatsoever. And yet for this man whom she had known only two weeks, who was nothing to her, she was ready to hate her sister, the person she had loved best of all, whom she still loved. . . . (No! . . . Yes! . . . whom she still loved. . . .) To this man she had sacrificed, offhand, all the rest of her life. . . . But how . . . how could that be possible! . . .

She was aghast; but she could only admit the omnipotence of her madness. At certain moments a flash of good sense, an ironical start, a returning wave of her old affection for Sylvie would lift her head above the stream. But a jealous glance, the sight of Tullio whispering with Sylvie, was enough to plunge her back again. . . .

It was obvious that she was losing ground. It was precisely for that reason that her passion was maddened. She was clumsy. Annette did not know how to hide her wounded dignity. Tullio, kindly prince, had consented not to choose between them; he deigned to toss his handkerchief to both. Sylvie picked it up in a trice; she did not stand on ceremony; later she would make Tullio dance to her liking. She was not bothered when she saw this Don Juan snatching a few kisses from Annette in the arbor. And even if it had displeased her, she saw no reason why she had to show it. One could dissimulate. . . . But Annette was incapable of it. She would countenance no division of favors, and she allowed herself to show only too plainly the repulsion which Tullio's equivocal play aroused in her.

Tullio was beginning to cool towards her. This serious passion embarrassed him, bored him. A little seriousness in love is all right. But not too much; that makes it a burden, and not a pleasure. He thought of passion as a prima donna who, after singing her great cavatina, returns with extended arms to salute the public. But Annette's passion did not seem to know that the public existed. She played only for herself. She played badly. . . .

She was too sincere, too truly in love to remove the traces of her suffering, of her torments, and those ordinary blemishes that a more attentive woman effaces or mitigates more than once a day. She did not appear at all to advantage. She became even homely, in the measure that she felt herself beaten.

The triumphant Sylvie, sure of her victory, watched the disabled Annette with ironical satisfaction, spiced with a grain of malice, and, at bottom, a little pity. . . .

"Well, have you had enough? Is that what you wanted? You're certainly a sight! . . . A poor beaten dog. . . ."

And she wanted to run and hug her. But when she approached, Annette displayed so much animosity that Sylvie turned her back in vexation, grumbling:

"You don't want me to, my girl? . . . Have it your own way! Look after yourself! I'm all right! . . . Everyone for himself, and that for the others! After all, if the fool is suffering, it's her own fault! Why is she always so ridiculously serious?"

(That was what they were all thinking.)

Annette ended by withdrawing from the combat. Sylvie and Tullio were getting up a program of tableaux, in which Sylvie could show off all her charms, and a few more besides. . . . (She was a little Parisian magician who, with a shred of material, could transform herself into a series of "doubles," all much prettier than the original, but which, by completing that original, made it appear more charming than them all, since it gave birth to them all.) . . . To try to fight her on this ground would have been disastrous for Annette. She knew it only too well: she was beaten in advance; what would she have been afterwards? She asked to be left out of the entertainment, giving her health as an excuse: her ill appearance was excuse enough. And Tullio did not insist. Scarcely had she refused when she suffered the more at having retired fully armed from the battle. Even when hope is dead, a struggle engenders fresh hope. Now she had to leave Tullio and Sylvie alone together for a part of the day. In order to embarrass them she obliged herself to attend all the rehearsals. She didn't embarrass them much. On the contrary she stimulated them, especially that brazen girl, who insisted on rehearsing ten times a scene that showed the abduction of a fainting odalisque by a Byronian corsair with eyes of sombre fire, gnashing teeth,—fatal, feline, ready to leap like a jaguar. Tullio played the rôle as though he were

going to put the whole Palace Hotel to fire
and sword.   As for Sylvie, she might have
given points to the twenty thousand houris
who hold the Prophet's beard in Paradise.

The evening of the performance arrived.
Annette, hidden away in the last row of
the hall, happily forgotten in the midst
of the enthusiasm, could not stay until the
end.   She left in torture.   Her head was
afire; her mouth was bitter; she was chewing the cud of her suffering.   Love scorned
was gnawing at her vitals.

She went into the fields that surrounded
the hotel; but she could not go far away,
she kept circling around that lighted hall.
The sun had set, darkness was falling.
With an animal instinct she smelled out the
door by which the two would certainly
make their exit; a little side door that
enabled the actors, without coming through
the hall, to regain the dressing rooms in
another wing of the building.   They ac-
tually did come out, and before they had
gone far they lingered in the shadow of
the field to talk.   Hidden behind a clump

of trees, Annette could hear Sylvie laughing, laughing . . .

"No, no, not to-night!"

And Tullio was insisting: "Why not?"

"First of all, I want to sleep."

"There's plenty of time to sleep!"

"No, no, never enough! . . ."

"Well then, to-morrow night."

"It's the same for the other nights. And then I'm not alone at night; I'm spied on."

"Then it will never be?"

And that little rascal of a Sylvie replied, twisting with laughter:

"But I'm not afraid of the daylight! Are you afraid of it? . . ."

Annette could listen no longer. A storm of disgust, fury, and unhappiness swept her away, running, into the night, into the fields. Perhaps they heard the noise of her mad flight and the crackling of branches, like that which follows on the heels of a fleeing animal. But she no longer cared whether she was heard or not. Nothing mattered any more. She was fleeing, fleeing. . . . Whither? She did not know.

She never knew. . . . She ran through the
night, moaning. She did not see ahead of
her. She ran on for five minutes, twenty
minutes, an hour? She never knew how
long. . . . Until her foot struck a root,
and she fell full length, her head against a
tree trunk. . . . And then she screamed,
she howled, with her mouth against the
ground, like a wounded beast.

Around her, the night. A sky without
moon or stars, black. A mute earth, untroubled by a breath or by the cries of in-
sects. Only the sound of a trickle of water
over the pebbles, dripping at the foot of
the slim fir against which Annette had
struck her forehead. And from the depths
of the gorge that cut the high, abrupt
plateau, there rose the fierce rumbling of
a mountain stream. Its plaint mingled
with the plaint of the wounded woman.
They seemed the eternal *lamento* of the
earth. . . .

So long as she cried, she did not think.
Her body, shaken by convulsive sobs, was
ridding itself of the burden of evil that

had crushed it down for days. The mind was silent. Then the body, exhausted, ceased to moan. Mental misery rose to the surface. And Annette again became conscious of her forsakenness. She was alone and betrayed. The circle of her thoughts could stretch no further. She had not the strength to reassemble their dispersed company. She had not even the strength to get up. Stretched out, she abandoned herself to the earth. . . . Oh! if only the earth wished to take her! . . . The rumbling of the mountain stream was speaking, thinking for her.

It was bathing her wound. After a period (long, no doubt) of prostrate suffering, Annette slowly raised her stricken body. The bruise on her forehead pained her sharply enough, and preoccupation with this hurt eased her mind. She dipped her scratched hands in the rivulet, she pressed them against her wounded, burning forehead. And so she remained seated, her eyes and forehead sunk in her wet palms, feeling the penetration of that icy purity. . . . And her grief became a distant thing.

. . . She observed its moaning as might a stranger; and she no longer understood the meaning of those transports. She was thinking:

"Why? . . . What's the good? . . . Is it worth the pain? . . ."

And in the night the torrent answered:

"Folly, folly, folly . . . all is vain . . . all is nothing . . ."

And Annette smiled a bitter smile of pity.

"What was it that I wanted? . . . I don't even know, any more. . . . Where is it, that great happiness? Take it who will. . . . . I shall not dispute it. . . ."

And then suddenly there returned to her in waves pictures of that happiness that she had desired, hot gusts of those desires by which her body was, and for a long time would be, possessed, even while her reason denied them. In the path traced by their bitter goad, they trailed after them a musty smell of jealous rages. . . . She suffered their attack in silence, bent over as beneath the wing of a passing wind. Then, raising her head, she said aloud:

"I have been wrong. . . . It is Sylvie he loves. . . . That is as it should be. She is better made for love. She is much prettier. I know it, and I love her. I love her because she is so. So I should be happy in her happiness. I am an egotist. . . . Only why, why has she lied to me? All the rest, but not that! Why has she deceived me? Why didn't she tell me frankly that she loved him? Why has she treated me like an enemy? Oh! And then all those things about her that I would rather not see, that are not very nice, not very good, not very beautiful! . . . But she is not to blame. How could she know? What a life she must have led from childhood! And have I the right to reproach her? . . . Were the feelings that I had any nicer? . . . That I had? That I have! . . . I know perfectly well that they are still there. . . ."

She sighed, worn out. Then she said:

"Come, this must end! I am the elder. And the greater folly is mine! . . . Let Sylvie be happy!"

But after having said, "Come," she still

remained for a while without stirring. She hearkened to the silence and dreamed, sucking the knuckles of her bruised fingers. And then she sighed, stood up without a word, and began to walk.

XII

She was returning, through the night.
The moon had not yet appeared; it was
still far off, but one could feel it rising
behind the horizon, from an abyss of
shadows. A feeble light edged the sum-
mits that encircled the plateau like the
edges of a cup; and, minute by minute,
their black profiles grew clearer against an
aureoled background. Annette walked unhurriedly; and her breast, breathing regu-
larly once more, was drinking in the scent
of new-mown meadows.

Far off in the darkness, she heard pre-
cipitate steps upon the road. Her heart
pounded. She halted. She recognized
them, and then walked forward again, at a
quicker pace, to meet them. Someone had
heard on the other side, too. An anxious
voice called:

"Annette!"

Annette did not reply, she could not;
she was seized with the joy that coursed

141

through her: all of her suffering, all was effaced. She did not answer, but she walked faster, still faster. And the other was running now. She repeated, "Annette!" in an agonized voice.

In the vague phosphorescence of the moon, that was climbing up behind the great dark wall, an indistinct figure emerged from the whitening shadow. Annette cried, "Darling!" and flung herself forward with outstretched arms, like a blind person. . . .

In their haste to be united, their bodies collided. Their arms went around each other. Their lips sought, and found . . .

"My own Annette!"

"My own Sylvie!"

"My sister! my love!"

"My little darling!"

In the darkness they were running their hands caressingly over cheeks and hair, over neck and shoulders, once more taking possession of happiness, of the friend who had been lost.

"Darling!" exclaimed Sylvie, feeling

Annette's bare shoulders, "you haven't your cloak! You have nothing around you! . . ."

Annette realized that as a matter of fact she was clad only in her evening dress; and, seized by a chill, she shivered.

"You are mad! you are mad!" cried Sylvie, enveloping her, clasping her in her cape. And her hands, continuing their inspection, took note of damages.

"Your dress is torn. . . . What in the world have you been doing? What has happened? . . . And your hair is down over your face. And here, here, what's the matter with your forehead? . . . Annette, did you fall? . . ."

Annette did not respond. With her mouth on Sylvie's shoulder, she abandoned herself and wept. Sylvie made her sit down beside her on a bank by the road. The moon, clearing the barrier of the mountains, lighted up Annette's injured forehead, and Sylvie covered it with kisses.

"Tell me what you have been doing. . . . Tell me what's happened. . . . My treasure, my little lamb, I was so upset when I went to your room and didn't find you there! I called you everywhere. . . . I've been hunting for you for an hour. . . . Oh! I was so miserable. . . . I was afraid, I was afraid. . . . I can't say what I was afraid of. . . . Why did you go off? Why did you run away? . . ."

Annette did not wish to reply.

"I don't know," she said. "I felt ill, and I wanted to walk . . . to breathe. . . ."

"No, you aren't telling the truth, Annette; tell me everything!"

Then she bent over her and said more softly:

"Dear heart, it wasn't because of that? . . ."

Annette interrupted her:

"No! No!"

But Sylvie insisted.

"Don't lie! Tell me the truth. Tell me! Tell your little one! It was because of him?"

Annette, wiping her eyes and trying to smile, replied:

"No, I assure you. . . . I was a little hurt, it's true. . . . It's foolish. . . . But it's all over now.   I'm glad he loves you."

Sylvie jumped up and struck her hands angrily together.

"So it was he!   Oh!   But I don't love him, I don't love him any more, that creature! . . ."

"Yes, you do love him. . . ."

"No!   No!   No!"

Sylvie stamped on the road.

"It amused me to love him, I did it as a game; but it meant nothing to me, nothing in comparison with you. . . . Why! All a man's kisses couldn't make up for one of your tears. . . ."

Annette was overwhelmed with happiness.

"You mean it?   You mean it?"

Sylvie sprang into her arms.

When they had grown somewhat calmer, Sylvie said to Annette:

"Now confess!   You loved him, too!"

"Too!   Now you see!   You admit that you loved him. . . ."

"No, I tell you.   I forbid you to say so. . . . I won't hear any more about it. It's ended, ended."

"It's ended," Annette repeated.

They went back along the road bathed in the light of the moon, overjoyed at having recovered each other. Suddenly Sylvie halted, and, shaking her fist at the moon, she cried:

"Oh! the beast! . . . He'll pay me for it!"

And, as youth never loses its rights, she burst out laughing at her malediction.

"But do you know what we are going to do?" Sylvie continued spitefully. "We are going to pack as soon as we get back, and to-morrow, to-morrow morning, we'll be off by the first post. When he comes to the table at luncheon time, he'll find no one. . . . The birds will have flown! . . . Oh! . . . and then . . ." (she burst out laughing) "I made a date with him for about ten o'clock, in the woods up there. . . . He'll be running after me all morning. . . ."

She laughed more heartily than ever; and so did Annette. The spectacle of Tullio, disappointed and furious, seemed so amusing to them. The two madcaps! Already their sufferings were far away.

"Just the same," observed Annette, "it's not very nice, dear, to compromise yourself like that."

"Piffle! What's that to me?" replied Sylvie. "I don't matter. . . . Yes," she went on, taking a passing nip at Annette's hand that was patting her ear, "I should be more careful now that I'm your sister. . . . I will be, I promise you. . . . But you, my dear, you know that you weren't so much more careful."

"No, that's true," answered Annette contritely. "And I was afraid at times that I might be still less so. . . . Oh!" she exclaimed, pressing closer to her sister, "how strange the heart is! One never, never knows when it's going to rise up inside you and carry you away . . . whither?"

"Yes," said Sylvie, hugging her, "that's why I love you! That heart of yours is a powerful affair!"

They were ready to go in again. The roofs of the hotel were gleaming under the moonlight. Sylvie slipped her arm around Annette's neck and whispered in her ear with an intensity and a seriousness she herself did not realize:

"My darling! I shall never forget what you have suffered to-night . . . what you have suffered because of me. . . . Yes, yes, don't say no! I had time to think of it while I was running in search of you, trembling that some misfortune . . . If it had happened! . . . Oh! what would I have done! . . . I should have never come back."

"Darling," exclaimed Annette, deeply moved, "it was not your fault, you couldn't know how you were hurting me."

"I knew perfectly well. I knew that I was making you suffer, and it—listen, Annette!—it even gave me pleasure!"

Annette's heart contracted; and a short while ago she too had thought that she would like to make Sylvie suffer until the blood ran. She said so. They clasped each other in their arms.

"But what's the matter with us? What are we?" they asked each other, shamefaced and stricken, yet relieved to know that the other's feelings had been the same. . . .

"It was love," said Sylvie.

"Love," Annette repeated mechanically. Then she went on, frightened:

"That is love?"

"And you know," said Sylvie, "it was only the beginning."

Annette protested vigorously that she never wanted to love again.

Sylvie made fun of her. But Annette repeated in perfect seriousness:

"I don't want to any more. I'm not made for it."

"Oh, well," said Sylvie, laughing, "there's not a chance, my poor Annette! You, why you'll stop loving when you stop living!"

ANNETTE AND SYLVIE

PART TWO

I

FIRST days of October, gray and sweet. Still air. Warm rain falling straight down, unhurriedly. The hot and fleshly odor of moist earth, ripe fruits in the cellar, vatsful in the cider press. . . .

Near an open window in the Rivière's country house, in Burgundy, the two sisters were sitting opposite each other, sewing. With heads bent over their work, they seemed to be pointing their round, smooth foreheads at each other,—the same rounded forehead, prettier in Sylvie, stronger in Annette, capricious in the one, obstinate in the other,—the goat and the little bull. But when they raised their heads, their eyes exchanged an understanding glance. Their tongues were resting, having chimed away for entire days. They were ruminating on their fever, their transports, the hosts of words that had passed between them, and all that they had acquired and learned from each other during the preceding days. For this time they had given themselves completely, eager to take all and give all. And now they were silent, the better to think of all this hidden booty.

But they had desired in vain to see all and to possess all: in the last analysis, each remained an enigma to the other. And to every human being, no doubt, every other human being is an enigma; and that is an attraction. How many things there were in each that the other would never understand! And they said truly (for they knew it):

"Of what importance is understanding? To understand is to explain. One doesn't have to explain in order to love. . . ."

But all the same, it makes considerable difference! It amounts to this, that without understanding one cannot possess completely. And then as regarded loving, precisely how did they love? They had not at all the same way of loving. Raoul Rivière's two daughters both inherited, undoubtedly, an abundant vigor from their

father, but it was concentrated in the one
and dispersed in the other. In nothing
were the two sisters more different than in
love. Sylvie's affection was perfectly un-
restrained, laughing, gamin-like, impudent,
but at bottom extremely sensible; she was
always on the move, but she never lost her
sense of direction, always fluttering her
wings, but never flying beyond the pigeon
yard. In Annette there dwelt a strange
demon of love, of whose presence she had
been aware for scarcely six months; she
suppressed it, endeavoured to hide it, for
she was afraid of it; her instinct told her
that others would misunderstand it: Eros
caged, with blindfolded eyes, troubled, hungry and starving, silently bruising himself
against the bars of the world, and slowly
gnawing away the heart in which he is
imprisoned! The burning, incessant, noise-
less, biting pain insensibly plunged Annette's mind into a confused, wounded
lethargy, that was not wholly unpleasant,
for she found a certain pleasure in the sensations that caused her suffering: it was like
being wrapped in a rough-surfaced mate-

rial, turned wrong side out, or like running one's hand over the harsh surface of a piece of furniture or the chill of a rugose wall. Chewing the bitter bark of some twig that she was nibbling, she would sink at times into a forgetfulness of self and time, into lapses of consciousness that lasted Heaven knows how long,—a quarter of a second or an hour? And she would precipitately pull herself out of them, suspicious and ashamed, sensing the invisible gaze of Sylvie upon her, for her sister while pretending to work was maliciously spying on her from the corner of her eye. Without understanding it very well, Sylvie with her little nose smelled out this inner life of Annette's that was sleeping in the sun and coiling itself, with sharp warnings, like an adder beneath the leaves. She thought that her big sister was very strange, a little cracked, really different from other people. . . . She was not so much astonished by Annette's passionate movements, her ardors, and what she could guess of her troubled thoughts, as by the almost tragic seriousness with which Annette invested them. Tragic?

What an idea! Serious? Why be that?
Things are as they are. One takes them as
they are. Sylvie was not going to bother
herself about the fifteen hundred notions
that passed through her head! They come,
and then they go away. Everything that's
nice and agreeable is simple and natural;
and everything that isn't nice and agreeable
is just as natural, too. Nice or not nice,
I swallow them: they are soon down!
Why make such a fuss? . . . Poor Annette, all tangled up! with her bundles of
hot and cold thoughts, her snarl of fears
and desires, and her clusters of passions
and decencies all mixed up in every corner!
. . . Who will untangle her? But the fact
that she was so abnormal, exaggerated and
incomprehensible amused and attracted Sylvie greatly; and she loved her only the
better for it. . . .

The prolonged silence was heavy with
disquieting secrets. Sylvie would abruptly
break it, and begin to talk at random. . . .
Quickly, very quickly, and in a low voice,
with her nose over her work as though she
were reviling it, she would begin to mutter

a litany of crazy little words, of inarticulate sounds, generally in *i*,—the *kikikiki* of
a chaffinch wriggling with delight. And
then, presto, she would again assume, a
serious expression, as if to say: "Who? I?
I didn't do anything. . . ." Or, nibbling
her thread, she would sing in her thin,
nasal voice some silly ballad that had to do
with flowers and "twittering birds," or a
snatch of an obscene song from which she
would select a particularly racy bit, with
the air of a wise child. And Annette would
start up, half-laughing, half-annoyed, and
exclaim:

"Will you please be good enough to shut
up!"

But they would be relieved. The air
was cleared. Words matter little; voices,
like hands, reestablish contact. They were
united again. Where were we? . . . Beware of silence! Do we know where it
may carry you, carry me, with the flutter
of a wing, in a moment of forgetfulness?
Speak to me! I am talking to you. I am
holding you. Hold me tight! . . .

They held on to each other. They were

firmly decided that whatever happened they would not let go again. Whatever happened, it would in no wise affect the essential fact: "I am I. You are you. We accept each other. Agreed! There's no going back." It was a mutual gift, a tacit contract, a kind of soul marriage, much more efficacious than any external bond; neither written engagement, nor religious or civil sanction could outweigh it. And what did it matter that they were so different? It is a mistake to think that the best unions are founded on affinities,—or even on contrasts. They are founded on neither one nor the other, but on an inner act, on an "I have chosen, I wish, I vow," of good metal and solidly stamped with the mark of an inflexible dual decision, as in the case of these two girls with rounded foreheads. "I have you, and I am no more able to give you back than to take myself back. . . . Besides you are free to love whom you choose, to do what you please . . . you may commit any folly, even a little crime if you have to (I know that you won't! but just the same!)—it will not affect our pact in any way. . . ." Explain it who will! Scrupulous Annette, if she had dared to follow her thought to its conclusion, would have been forced to confess that she was not quite sure of Sylvie's moral worth or of her future actions. And clear-sighted Sylvie would not have staked her hand that Annette would not, some day, be capable of disconcerting acts. But this had to do with others, it did not concern them, the two of them. As for themselves, they were sure, they had an absolute confidence in each other. The rest of the world could manage its affairs as it pleased! No matter what either might do—since it could not affect their mutual love—they forgave everything in advance, with closed eyes.

Perhaps it was not very moral, but what of that! They would have time to be moral on some other occasion.

Annette who was a bit of a pedant, who knew life through books—which did not however keep her from discovering it later (for life has not quite the same ring when it is heard outside of books)—Annette remembered those beautiful verses of Schiller's:

"Oh, my sons, the world is full of lies and of hatred; everyone loves himself alone; all bonds formed by a fragile happiness are insecure. . . . That which caprice has joined together, that will caprice put asunder. Nature alone is sincere, it alone rests upon unshakable anchors. All else floats at the will of stormy waves. . . . Inclination gives you a friend, interest a companion; happy is he to whom birth has given a brother. . . . Against this world of war and treachery, they are two to stand together. . . ."

Sylvie did not know these verses, that is certain! And, no doubt, she would have thought that they employed entirely too many confused words for the expression of a simple sentiment. But as she looked at Annette, who was not working now, at her bowed head, the firm nape of her neck, and her heavy mass of twisted hair, she thought:

"She is still dreaming, the big dear; she is deep again in her chest of follies. What that chest must hold! It's lucky that I'm

here, now!   It won't be opened without
me. . . ."

For the younger sister had a conviction,
perhaps exaggerated, of her superior sense
and experience.   And she said to herself:
"I shall protect her."

She might have needed to protect herself
first; for in her own chest there was no
lack of follies either.   But she knew all
about these in advance, and she regarded
them as a landlord regards his tenants.   If
one lodges them, it is not for nothing. . . .
And then, "Do what you wish, come what
may!"   So long as it concerned only herself
it was not of enormous importance.   One
could always find a way out. . . . But to
protect someone else, that was a new and
delectable feeling. . . .

Yes, but . . .   Annette, with her head
bowed and her hands idle, was cherishing
precisely the same feeling.   She was thinking: "My dear little madcap! . . . It's
lucky that I came along in time to look
after her! . . ."

And for Sylvie's future she made plans
that were certainly charming, but con-

cerning which Sylvie had not been consulted. . . .

Then when each had thoroughly pondered the happiness of the other (and her own into the bargain, of course.) . . .

"Hang! my needle is broken. . . . One can't see a thing any more. . . ." They threw aside their work and went outdoors together to stretch their legs; both wrapped in the same greatcoat, they walked through the rain to the end of the gardēn, beneath weeping trees whose locks were falling; from the arbor they plucked a bunch of white grapes, all the better for being moist; they talked, and they talked. . . . And then suddenly they fell silent, drinking in the autumn wind, the delectable odor of fallen fruits, of dead leaves, and the tired October light that faded at four o'clock, the silence of the numbed, slumbering fields, the earth drinking up the rain, the night . . .

And, hand in hand, they dreamed with quivering Nature, that brooded over the fearful, burning hope of spring,—the enigma of the future. . . .

II

During those fine, foggy October days, when the fog rolled up like a spider's web, their intimacy became so necessary to them that they wondered how they had ever done without it.

Yet they had done without it, and they would again. Life, at the age of twenty, does not confine itself to a single intimacy, however dear it may be,—especially the life of two such winged creatures. They must essay the airy spaces. Firm as the affirmation of their heart's desire may be, the instinct of their wings is stronger. When Annette and Sylvie said to each other tenderly: "How could we have lived so long without each other?" they did not confess to themselves, "But sooner or later (what a pity!) we shall have to live without each other again!"

For another cannot live for you, in your place; and you would not wish it. Assuredly the need of their mutual affection

164

was profound, but the two little Rivières felt another, stronger need, that went deeper, to the very sources of their being: the need of independence. They who had so many different traits had precisely this trait in common (it was not by chance!). And they were perfectly aware of it; it was even one of the reasons for which, without saying so, they loved each other the more; for in it each saw herself. But then, what would become of their plans to fuse their two lives? While each was cradling herself in a dream that she might protect the other's life, she knew that the other would consent to it no more than she herself would consent. It was a fond dream with which they played. They were trying to make the play last as long as possible.

And yet it could not last for long.

It would have amounted to nothing had they both been merely independent. But these two little Republics, that were so jealous of their freedom, had, without realizing it, like all Republics, despotic instincts. As each considered its own laws excellent, each had a tendency to export

them to the other. Annette, who was capable of self-criticism, would blame herself when it was too late for trampling upon
her sister's domain,—but then she would do
it all over again. Hers was a willful and
passionate character, which, despite herself,
was inclined to dominate. Her nature was
quite capable of temporary weakness, beneath the veil of a great affection, but it
remained unchanged. It must be confessed,
besides, that if Annette made an effort to
adapt herself to Sylvie's wishes, Sylvie did
not make the task easy for her. All her
actions were headstrong, and within twenty-
four hours her head had more than twenty-
four whims, that were not always mutually
compatible. Annette, who was methodical
and orderly, laughed at first and after that
grew impatient at these sudden shifts and
caprices. She called Sylvie *Rose of the
Winds*, and *I want . . . What is it I
Want?* And Sylvie called her *Squall*,
Madame I Ordain, and *Noon at Twelve
Sharp*, because she was plagued by Annette's
punctuality.

Even while they were devoted to each
other, it was difficult for them to accom-
modate themselves for very long to the same
manner of living. They had neither the
same tastes nor the same habits. Because
they loved each other, Annette could lend
an indulgent ear to the little splutterings of
Sylvie, who had an excellent eye for the
main chance, and a still better ear, but not
a very good tongue. And Sylvie, swallow-
ing an amused yawn ("Get along! Will
you get along! . . .), was capable of appearing interested in the deadly reading, the
pleasure of which Annette wished to share
with her. . . .

"My! how pretty that is, dear!"

Or, commenting to herself on certain
preoccupations with ridiculous thoughts on
life, death, or society . . .

(What a bore! . . . Tootle-too-too! . . .
They have plenty of time to waste! . . .)

"And you," Annette would ask, "what
do you think of it, Sylvie?"

("Piffle!" thought Sylvie.)

"I think the same as you do, dear."

This in no wise prevented them from adoring each other; but at the same time it somewhat hampered their conversation.

And what could they do with their days, alone in the sombre house by the edge of the woods, confronted by stripped fields, under a low autumn sky that mingled with the bare plain in the fog?   In vain had Sylvie asserted and believed that she adored the country; she had soon exhausted its pleasures, and in the country she was idle, out of place, lost. . . . Nature, nature. . . . Let us be frank!   Nature bored her. . . . A land of rustics!   No!   She could not bear the little inclemencies: wind, rain, mud (the mud of Paris, in comparison, seemed pleasant to her), the mice trotting up and down behind old partitions, the spiders who came indoors to take up their winter quarters, and those frightful beasts, the buzzing mosquitoes, who regaled themselves on her wrists and ankles.   She could have wept with irritation and boredom. Annette, rejoicing in the open air and in the solitude with her beloved sister, invulnerable to boredom, laughing at mosquito

bites, tried to drag Sylvie along on her
muddy walks, without noticing her sullen,
disgusted expression. A gust of wind and
rain intoxicated her; forgetting Sylvie, she
would set off with great strides over the
plowed earth or through the woods, shaking the wet branches; and it was not until
long after that she remembered the little
straggler. And Sylvie, who was sulking and
piteously examining her swollen face, would
wait vainly, thinking:

"When are we going back?"

But among the thousand and one desires
of the younger Rivière girl, there was one
that was good and praiseworthy, that nothing could alter, and the country air served
only to lend it new lustre. She loved her
trade. She really loved it. Of good Parisian working stock, work was necessary to
her; she needed her needle and her thimble
to busy her fingers and her thoughts. She
had an innate love of sewing; it was a
physical pleasure for her to spend hours
handling some piece of material, a dainty
fabric, a silk muslin, folding it, gathering
it, giving a touch to a knot of ribbons.

And then her little noddle, which did not flatter itself, Heaven be praised, that it understood the ideas lodged in Annette's big brain, knew that here in her own domain, in the kingdom of chiffons, she had ideas too, enough and to spare. . . . Well then, could she give up her ideas? It is thought that a woman can enjoy no greater pleasure than to wear pretty dresses! . . . For a really gifted woman it is a much greater pleasure to make them. And once one has tasted this pleasure, one cannot forego it. In the downy idleness in which her sister kept her, while Annette was running her hands over the piano keys, Sylvie felt homesick for the noise of big shears and the sewing machine. All the works of art in the world, had they been offered to her, would not have made up for the fine, headless dummy that one can drape according to one's fancy, that one can twist and turn, before which one squats, that one slyly maltreats, and that one takes in one's arms for a dance when the forewoman is absent. A few casual words sufficiently indicated the drift of her thoughts; and impatient

Annette, seeing her eyes light up, knew that she was in for another story of the shop.

So when Sylvie announced, after their return to Paris, that she was going back to her lodging and her regular work, Annette sighed; but she was not surprised. Sylvie, who had expected opposition, was much more touched by this sigh, by this silence, than she would have been by any words. She ran to her seated sister, and, kneeling before her, she clasped her arms around her waist and held her mouth up to her.

"Annette, don't be angry with me!"

"Darling," Annette replied, "your happiness is mine, and you know it."

But she was suffering, and Sylvie was too.

"It is not my fault," she protested. "I love you tremendously, I swear!"

"Yes, dearest, I know that."

Annette was smiling, but she heaved another deep sigh. Sylvie, still on her knees, took her sister's face between her hands and put her own close to it.

"I forbid you to sigh! . . . Villain! If

you sigh like that I sha'nt be able to leave.
I'm not a little wretch."

"No, darling, you aren't. . . . It was
wrong of me, and I won't do it any more.
But I wasn't blaming you. It's because we
are leaving each other."

"Leaving each other! . . . The idea!
. . . Naughty girl! We shall see each
other every day. You will come, and I
shall come. You will keep my room for
me. Were you going to presume, by any
chance, to take it away from me? No, no,
it's mine, and I won't give it back. When
I am tired, I count on coming here to be
petted. And you know, some evenings
when you aren't expecting me, I shall arrive at the most unreasonable hours; I have
a key, I shall come in and surprise you.
. . . Beware if you play any tricks! . . .
You will see, you will see, we shall love
each other all the better. . . . Leave each
other! Do you think that I would want to
leave you, that I could get along without
my pretty Annette!"

"Oh! the wheedler, the little rascal!"
said Annette, laughing, "how well she

knows how to cajole one! The damned little liar!"

"Annette! Don't swear!" exclaimed Sylvie severely.

"Well then, simply liar. . . . Is that all right?"

"Yes, that may pass," replied Sylvie magnanimously. . . .

She threw herself on Annette's neck and suffocated her with kisses.

"Lie to you, lie to you, I'm eating you! . . ."

The affectionate, cunning girl had other ways of winning forgiveness. She asked Annette to help her set up shop on her own account. This "lass" of twenty wanted to be her own mistress, to take orders no longer, to give orders in her turn,—if only to her dummy. Annette was delighted at being able to give her money. The two sisters put their heads together, endlessly discussed arrangements, ran about the following day to find a place, then to choose furniture and materials, then to arrange matters with the authorities; and they spent the evenings making up lists of customers, making plan after plan, move after move, —until Annette ended by having the illusion that it was she who was setting up shop with Sylvie. And she forgot that their lives were going to be divorced.

III

Customers were not slow in coming to
Sylvie's. When Annette went calling, she
wore the little dressmaker's prettiest crea-
tions, and sang her praises. She succeeded
in sending to her many young women from
her own set. Sylvie, for her part, had no
scruples about exploiting the addresses of
her old employer's customers. However,
she was wise enough not to enlarge the
circle of her operations too rapidly. Little
by little. Life is long. There is plenty of
time. . . . She loved work, but not to the
mad degree of certain human ants—and
especially feminine ones—whom she had
seen kill themselves at their task. She had
every intention of leaving time for pleasure.
Work is one of them, but it is not the only
one. "*A little of everything.*" Hers was
the motto of a small appetite, but dainty
and curious. . . .

Before long her life was so filled that
not much of it remained for Annette.

Whatever happened, Sylvie guarded Annette's share; she clung to it. But for
Annette's heart, a share was little. She
did not know how to give herself in halves,
or thirds, or quarters. She still had to
learn that in their affections people are like
a small merchant: they deliver them retail.
She was long in understanding this, still
longer in accepting it. As yet she had not
passed beyond the first lessons.

Without saying so, she suffered at seeing
herself eliminated, little by little, from
Sylvie's days. Sylvie was never alone any
more, at home or in her shop. She had
acquired a new sweetheart. Annette bowed
to the inevitable. Her love for her sister
now defended her against her old jealous
spite and severity of judgment. But it did
not defend her against melancholy. Sylvie,
who, despite her lightness, loved her sister
well enough to sense the pain she was
causing her, would occasionally tear herself
away from the farandole of her activities,
both business and pleasure; and suddenly,
in the midst of work or even a tête-à-tête,
she would drop the most pressing matters

and run off to Annette's. Then there was
a whirlwind of passing tenderness. At the
moment, Sylvie was no less full of affection
than Annette. But it passed; and when the
whirlwind carried Sylvie back to her business or her pleasures, filled with Annette,
Annette would sigh, grateful for the little
tempest of loving chatter, mad confidences,
and laughing embraces that had visited her,
but feeling more alone than ever and more
troubled.

Yet it was not interests that she lacked.
Her days were as full as Sylvie's.

Her life, her double life, intellectual and
social, that had been broken off since her
father's death, had resumed its natural
course. Her mental needs, which during
the past year had been crowded aside by the
needs of her heart, had now reawakened
stronger than ever. As much to fill the
hours left empty by Sylvie's absence, as
because the intelligence of a rich nature is
matured by experiences of the passional life,
she had again applied herself to her scien-
tific studies, and she was astonished to

find that she brought to them a clearer gaze than before. She became interested in biology, and planned a thesis on the origins of the æsthetic sentiment and its manifestations in nature.

She had also picked up the threads of her social life; she returned to the world that she had formerly frequented with her father. And she found in it a fresh pleasure: the pleasure of curiosity, of a greater sophistication that discovered, in people she had thought she knew, unexpected aspects of which she had not dreamed. There were other pleasures too, of a very different sort, some that one acknowledged, and others that one did not confess: the pleasure of pleasing; obscure forces of attraction (of repulsion too) that awake in us and around us magnetic relations which are established between minds and bodies, under cover of deceptive words; dumb possessive instincts that momentarily graze the even and monotonous surface of drawing-room thoughts, instincts that efface themselves, but which quiver beneath the surface. . . .

Yet society and work occupied only the smallest portion of her time. Never had Annette's life been so peopled as now when she was alone. Through the long evenings and night hours, when sleep tosses the mind back into wakefulness, with its hallucinatory thoughts, as the withdrawing tide leaves on the shore a myriad of organisms torn from the nocturnal abysses of ocean, —Annette contemplated the ebb and flow of her interior sea, and the littered shore. It was the great spring equinox.

A part of the forces that stirred within her were not new to her; but, as their energy increased tenfold, the mind became conscious of them with an exalted clarity. Their contradictory rhythms caused an intoxication of the heart, a vertigo. . . . It was impossible to grasp the order hidden in this confusion. The violent shock of sexual passion that, like a summer storm, had shaken Annette's heart, was leaving behind it a lasting perturbation. In vain had the memory of Tullio been effaced, the equilibrium of her being was for a long time shaken. The tranquillity of her life, the

absence of events, created an illusion for
Annette: she could have believed that nothing had happened, and could have easily
repeated the careless cry of those watchmen
in the fine Italian nights: *Tempo sereno!*
. . . But the hot night was hatching new
storms, and the unstable air was shivering
with disquiet eddies. A perpetual disorder.
The thrusts of dead souls, revivified, clashed
in this soul in fusion. . . . Here, the dangerous paternal heritage consisting of those
desires that were ordinarily dormant and
forgotten, rose abruptly like a wave from
the deep. There, opposing forces: a moral
pride, the passion for purity. And that
other passion for independence, the imperious constraint of which Annette had
already experienced in her union with Sylvie; she anxiously foresaw, too, that this
passion for independence would some day
engage in still more tragic conflicts with
love. All this inner travail occupied her,
filled her, during the long winter days.
The soul, like a chrysalis encased in a
cocoon of foggy light, was dreaming of

its future, and indulging itself in its
dream. . . .

Suddenly, she went beyond her depth.
There occurred one of those lapses of consciousness such as she had experienced last
autumn, here and there, in Burgundy; one
of those voids into which one sinks. . . .
Voids? No, they were not voids; but
what went on in their depths? Those
strange phenomena, unperceived, perhaps
non-existent until ten months before, that
had been released especially since the amorous crisis of the summer, and since then
had become more frequent. Annette had
a vague feeling that these gulfs of consciousness sometimes opened at night, too,
while she slept . . . the heavy sleep of
hypnosis. . . . When she came out of
them, she returned from a great distance;
there remained no memory of them, and
yet she had the haunting sense that she had
encountered important events and worlds,
unspeakable things, things beyond what the
reason permits and tolerates, bestial and
superhuman, reminiscent of the Greek mon-

sters or the cathedral gargoyles. A form-
less clay adhered to her fingers. One felt
oneself bound alive to that stranger of one's
dreams. There weighed a sorrow, a shame,
the fresh burden of a complicity that could
not be defined. One's skin remained im-
pregnated by an unsavory odor that lingered
for days. It was as though one bore a
secret, in the midst of the day's fugitive
images, hidden behind the closed door of a
smooth forehead unwrinkled by thought,
while one's indifferent eyes turned inward,
and one's hands lay sagely folded across
one's breast—a sleeping lake. . . . .

Wherever she went, Annette carried this
perpetual dream: in the bustle of streets, in
the studious torpor of lectures and libraries,
in the amiable banality of drawing-room
conversations, relieved by a hint of flirtation
and irony. At evening parties more than
one person noticed the absent glance of this
young girl who smiled distractedly, less at
what was said to her than at what she was
saying to herself, while she caught by
chance a few passing words, and then went
far away again, listening to no-one-knew-

what hidden birds in the depths of her aviary.

So noisy was the chorus of little people within Annette that one day she caught herself listening to it when Sylvie was with her,—Sylvie the beloved, laughing at her, deafening her with her dear chatter, saying to her. . . . What was it she was saying? . . . Sylvie perceived it, and she laughingly shook her.

"You're asleep, you're asleep, Annette!"

Annette protested.

"Yes, yes, I saw you, you are dreaming standing up, like an old carriage horse. What do you do with your nights?"

"Wretch! . . . And what about yours, if I asked you? . . ."

"Mine? You want to know? Very well! I'm going to tell you. You won't be bored."

"No! No!" exclaimed Annette, laughing, now thoroughly awake.

She clapped her hand over her sister's mouth. But Sylvie freed herself and, seizing Annette's head, looked straight into her eyes.

"Your beautiful sleep-walker's eyes. . . .
Show us a little of what's in there. . . .
What are you dreaming, Annette? Tell
me, tell me! Tell what you're dreaming.
Tell! Come along, let's hear!"

"What do you want me to tell?"

"Say what you are thinking about."

Annette resisted, but she always ended
by yielding. For both of them it was an
acute pleasure of affection, and perhaps of
egotism, to tell each other everything.
They left nothing out. So Annette tried
to unravel her dreams, much less for Sylvie's benefit than for her own comfort.
She explained, not without difficulty, but
with a great scrupulousness and seriousness
that made Sylvie burst into laughter, all
her mad thoughts—the innocent, the candid, the grotesque, the daring, and sometimes even . . .

"Well, well, Annette! I say, when you
try! . . ." exclaimed Sylvie, pretending to
be scandalized.

Her own inner life was perhaps no less
strange (neither more nor less than that of
all of us), but she did not suspect it, and

she was not interested in it, like a practical little person who believes once for all in what she sees and touches, in the sensible and ordinary dream of superficial earthly existence, and who avoids as absurd everything that might disturb it.

She laughed with all her heart, listening to her sister. Now who would ever have thought that of Annette! With her innocent air, she sometimes tells you the most egregious things in all seriousness. And then she is frightened at the simplest things, that everybody knows. (She shared them with Sylvie, with a comical conviction.) Heaven knows what ridiculous ideas are passing in her noddle! . . . Sylvie found her complicated, adorable, twisted, deucedly tangled up. Always that disease of being tormented to death by things that one should take as they come!

"The trouble is that they sing a half-a-dozen tunes at the same time," said Annette.

"Well, that's amusing," exclaimed Sylvie. "It's like the Lion de Béfort fair."

"Horrors!" cried Annette, stuffing up her ears.

"Why, I adore it. Three or four shooting galleries, tram horns, steam calliopes, bells, whistles, everyone yelling together, till one can't hear oneself think, while one yells louder than all of them,—and snorting, laughing and goings on that delight your heart. . . ."

"Little plebeian!"

"But, my little aristo, it's you (you've just said so), it's you who are like that! If you don't like it, you have only to do as I do. I have everything in order. Everything in its place. Every rabbit in its hutch!"

And indeed she spoke the truth. Whatever hubbub went on in the Place Denfert or in her own little brain, she knew how to manage in one case as well as the other. She could instantly bring order from the most inextricable disorder. She knew how to reconcile all her divers needs, both of mind and body, middle.class and otherwise. Each had its pigeon-hole. As Annette said to her:

"A bureau full of drawers. . . . That's what you are! . . ." (showing her the famous Louis XV chiffonier in which their father's letters had been arranged).

"Yes," replied Sylvie, "there *is* a resemblance. . . ."

(It was not of the piece of furniture that she spoke).

". . . At bottom, it's the *real me*. . . ."

She wanted to vex Annette. But Annette wasn't "rising" any more. She was no longer jealous of her father's heredity; she had her share of it. She could very well have given it up. It was, at times, a rather troublesome guest! . . .

IV

She did not know quite how, but during the past year she had lost the balance of her logical mind and of her stout legs that had been so firmly implanted in the real world; and she did not see how she was going to recover it. She would have given a good deal to put on Sylvie's little boots that unhesitatingly went clattering over the ground with their decided step. She no longer felt that she was bound firmly enough to ordinary life, to the life of everybody and every minute. Contrary to her sister, she was too much preoccupied with her inner existence, and she was not enough preoccupied, any more, with that on which the sun shone. It would, doubtless, have been the same, even had she not been caught by the great sexual trap into which dreamers fall more quickly and more clumsily than others. The insidious hour was approaching. The snare was being prepared. . . .

But would this snare, even, suffice to hold a rather wild soul and a thoroughbred for very long?. . .

While waiting to find out, she circled around,—certainly without realizing it, for if she had realized it she would have recoiled in exasperated revolt. No matter! Each of her steps brought her closer to the trap. . . .

She had to confess it to herself—she who, a year before, had affected to treat men with the calm assurance of a comrade; no doubt a little coquettish and amiable, but indifferent; for from them she had seemed neither to desire nor fear anything —she now looked on men with different eyes. She maintained an attitude of observation and troubled waiting. Since the adventure with Tullio, she had lost her fine, insolent calm.

She knew now that she could not get along without them; and her father's smile came to her lips when she recalled her childish declarations at the idea of marriage. Love had left its wasp's dart in her flesh. Chaste and burning, innocent and sophisticated, she knew her desires; and if she thrust them into the penumbra of her mind, they manifested their presence by the confusion into which they threw the remainder of her ideas. Her whole mental activity was disorganized. Her powers of reflection were paralyzed. At work, writing or reading, she felt herself somehow impaired. She could no longer concentrate on an object save at the cost of disproportionate effort; and afterwards she was exhausted, disgusted. And it was in vain, for the knot of her attention would always come undone. Clouds crept into all her thoughts. The perfectly clear—too clear and too well-lighted—goals that she had fixed for her intelligence, were dimmed in the fog. The straight road that was to lead her to them broke off, was cut at every step.

Annette discouragedly thought:

"I shall never get there."

Having formerly attributed to women all the intellectual powers of men, she experienced the humiliation of saying to herself:

"I was mistaken."

Under the impression of lassitude which oppressed her, she recognized (rightly or wrongly) certain cerebral weaknesses of her sex, due perhaps to woman's long unaccustomedness to disinterested thought, to that objective and detached activity of mind which is demanded by true science and true art; but more probably due to the mute obsession of those great, sacred instincts, the rich and heavy deposit of which nature has placed in her. Annette felt that, alone, she was incomplete; incomplete in mind, body and heart. But of these last two, she thought as little as possible; they recalled only too much to her mind.

She had reached the time of life when one can live no longer without a mate; and woman even less than man, for in her it is not only the lover, but the mother also, that is awakened by love. She does not realize it: the two aspirations are confounded in a single sentiment. Annette, as yet without defining a single one of her thoughts, had a heart swollen with the need of giving itself to some human being, at

once stronger and weaker than herself,
who would take her in his arms and who
would drink at her breast. At the thought
of this, she grew faint with tenderness;
would that all the blood in her body might
be turned to milk, that she might give
of it. . . . Drink! . . . Oh, my well beloved! . . .

Give all!. . . No! She could not give
all! It was not permitted her. Give all!
. . . Yes, her milk, her blood, her body,
and her love. . . . But all? her whole
soul? her whole will? and for her entire
life? . . . No, that, she was certain, she
could never do. Even when she wished
to, she would be unable. One cannot give
what is not one's own,—my free soul. My
free soul does not belong to me; it is I
who belong to my free soul. I cannot dis-
pose of it. . . . To conserve its liberty is
much more than a right, it is a religious
duty. . . .

There was in these thoughts of Annette
a little of the moral rigidity that she inherited from her mother. But in her, all
took on a passionate character; with her

impetuous blood she could give warmth to
the most abstract ideas. . . . Her "soul!"
. . . That "Protestant" word! . . . (It was
herself speaking. . . . She used the word
often! . . .) Had Raoul Rivière's daughter only one soul? She had a whole troop
of them, and in the lot there were three
or four of notable stature that did not always understand one another. . . .

Yet this internal conflict went on in an
undefined sphere. Annette had not yet had
the occasion to put her contrary passions to
the test. Their opposition was still a mental game that was ardent and sufficiently
stirring, but devoid of risks; she did not
have to decide; she could permit herself
the luxury of mentally trying one solution
or another.

It was a subject of laughing discussions
with Sylvie, one of those heart problems
that delight the heart of youth during
periods of idleness and waiting, until the
time comes when reality brusquely decides
for you, without bothering about your elegant arrangements. Sylvie perfectly understood Annette's double need; but, so far as

she was concerned, she could see no contradiction in it; one only had to do as she
did: love when it pleased you, be free when
it pleased you. . . .

But Annette shook her head.

"No!"

"Why not?"

She refused to explain.

And Sylvie asked mockingly:

"You think it's good enough for me?"

And Annette exclaimed:

"No, darling. You know perfectly well
that I love you, as you are."

But Sylvie was not far wrong. Through
affection, Annette (while she sighed to herself) refused to judge Sylvie's free loves.
But for herself she rejected the thought of
them. It was not merely the puritanism
inherited from her mother that would have
considered them dishonorable. It was her
"entire" nature, it was the very plenitude
of her Desire that refused to parcel itself
into small bits. Despite the obscure appeal
of a powerful sexual life, it would have
been impossible for her, at this moment of
her life, to receive without revolt the idea

of a love in which the whole being, senses, heart and thought, self-respect, respect for the other person, and the religious ardor of the impassioned soul, did not all equally have their places at the feast. To give her body and withhold her mind,—no, there could be no question of that. . . . It would be treachery! . . . Then there remained only one solution,—marriage, monogamous love? Was that a possible dream, for an Annette?

Possible or not, it cost nothing to dream it, in advance. She did not deprive herself of it. She had arrived at the edge of the wood of adolescence, at that beautiful, final instant when, still savoring the shadow and the shelter of dreams, one sees opening before one, on the plain, long white roads in the sunlight. On which shall we imprint out steps? There is no haste to choose. The mind laughingly delays, and it chooses them all. A happy young girl, without material cares, radiating love, her arms full of hope, sees offered to her heart the possibility of twenty different lives; and, even before asking herself, "Which do I pre-

fer?" she takes up the whole sheaf, to
breathe their sweetness. In imagination
Annette tasted, one by one, the future
shared with this and that, and then with
another, mate, dropping the bitten fruit,
nibbling at another, then returning to the
first, trying a third, without deciding on
any one. Age of uncertainty, at first happy
and exalted, but soon to know weariness,
crushing depression, and sometimes even
despairing doubt.

So Annette dreamed of her life,—of her
lives to come. To Sylvie alone she confided her uncertain waiting. And Sylvie
was amused at her sister's languorous, troubled indecision. She knew little about such
things, for it was her habit (she boasted of
it in order to scandalize Annette) to decide
before choosing. To decide immediately.
Afterwards, there was time to make one's
choice. . . .

"And at least," she said with her swag-
gering air, "one knows whereof one
speaks!"

V

In the society in which she moved, Annette was extremely successful. She was much sought after by the majority of the young men. The young girls, many of whom were prettier than she, did not take very kindly to this. They had the more reason to be galled because Annette did not seem to make any great effort to please. Distrait and a little distant, she did nothing to pique the interest or flatter the vanity of the men who sought her out. Calmly installed in a corner of the drawing-room, she let them come to her, without appearing to note their presence, listened smilingly (they were never sure that she had heard) and, when she answered, she uttered only pleasant commonplaces. However, they all came, and tried to charm her: the worldly, the brilliant, and the respectable young men.

The jealous ones liked to believe that Annette was playing a deep game, that her

indifference was only the ruse of a practised coquette; they remarked that for some
time now Annette's rather cold correctness
of dress had given place to elegant toilettes,
in which the fantastic note, they said, was
skilfully calculated to relieve the monot-
ony of her sleepy homeliness. Malicious
tongues added that it was her fortune more
than her face that was courted. But, as
regards the toilettes, their charming artifice
should not be attributed to Annette: Sylvie's
taste and wit were solely responsible. And,
no doubt, she was a "good catch," but if
her little court took cognizance of the fact,
as it surely did, it was only the nuance of
respect which marked their attentions that
might be attributed to this consideration.
Had she been less well provided by fortune, they would have pursued her no less
but more boldly.

The allurement was deeper. Annette,
without being a coquette, was well enough
served by her instincts. Rich and strong,
there was no need of anyone telling them
what had to be done; their action was sure,
for the will had no part in it. While An-

nette, smiling indolently as though submerged in her inner life, was allowing herself to be carried on the pleasant tide of a
vague revery, on a voluptuous wave, that
did not prevent her hearing and seeing,—
her body was speaking for her: a powerful
attraction was emanating from her eyes and
mouth and strong, young limbs, from the
youth of her being, charged with love like
a flowering glycine. The charm was so
strong that no one seeing her (at least, no
one but a woman) could dream that she
was homely. And if she spoke little, only
a few casual words are needed in an empty
conversation to evoke unusual mental horizons. Then too, she offered herself no less
to the desires of those who sought the soul,
than to the covetousness of those who had
recognized in this dormant body (sleeping
water) a wealth of pleasure unknown to
itself.

She did not seem to see; but she saw
perfectly well. It is a feminine gift. In
Annette it was complemented by a vigorous intuition which often goes with strong
vitality, and which, without words or ges-

tures, immediately penetrates the speech of
being to being. When she seemed distrait,
it meant that she was listening to this language. Dark forest of hearts! . . . They
were—they and she—on the hunt. Each
sought his track. Having drifted for a
time from one to another, Annette chose
her own.

The young men among whom her choice
lay belonged to that rich, intelligent, active
bourgeoisie, advanced in ideas (at least
they thought them advanced), of which.
Raoul Rivière had been a member. It was
shortly after the Dreyfus Affair, which
had brought together men belonging to
different orders of thought, who yet found
themselves united by a common instinct of
social justice. This instinct, as later became apparent, was not very enduring. So
far as it was concerned, social justice was
limited to a single injustice. One example
among thousands was Rivière himself, who
had lost no sleep over the iniquities of the
world, who had even been capable of con-
cluding with no pangs of conscience some
profitable business with the Sultan, when

His Highness was coolly engineering, amid
the silence of a complaisant Europe, the
first Armenian massacre,—yet who, quite
sincerely, had been completely bowled over
by the famous Affair. One cannot ask too
much of men! When they have fought
for justice, once in their lives, they are
winded. They have been just on at least
one occasion; one must be grateful for that.
They are grateful themselves. Rivière's
society, the families whose sons were now
Annette's suitors, had no doubt concerning
the merit they had acquired in the cham-
pionship of Right, nor concerning the in-
utility of refreshing this merit by new
efforts. They remained, once for all, the
crew of Progress, with folded arms.

With minds sufficiently at peace, besides,
as regarded the international landscape, in
this fleeting hour when civic conflicts had
nearly extinguished national hatreds—save
for the old ember of anglophobia, still kept
smoking by the Boer war,—possessed of a
diluted and not at all militaristic patriot-
ism,—given to tolerance and good humor,
because they were well off, belonging to the

victorious party,—they gave the impression
of an easy-going society, broad in its morality, vaguely humanitarian, more certainly
utilitarian and sceptical, with no very great
principles and no very great prejudices.
. . . (They need not have prided themselves on that! . . .) They counted in
their ranks a number of liberal Catholics,
not a few Protestants, a greater number of
Jews, and a quantity of solid middle-class
Frenchmen who were indifferent to all re-
ligions, having found a substitute in a political doctrine that bore various labels, but
did not stray very far from the republicanism which, having endured for thirty
years, was beginning to be a form, the most
practical form, of conservatism. Socialism,
too, was represented; but by the rich and
intellectual young bourgeois that had been
won over by the golden tongue and example
of Jaurès. He was still on his honeymoon
with the Republic.

Annette was never seriously interested in
politics. Her active inner life left her no
time for it. But, like the others, she had
passed through her hours of exaltation dur-

ing the Affair.   Her love for her father
modeled her in the image of his feelings.
She was predisposed, by the fire in her
heart and by the instinct of liberty that she
carried in her blood, to find herself always
on the side of the oppressed.   So she had
known moments of passionate emotion when
Zola and Picquart faced the great Beast—
unchained public opinion; and it is not impossible that, like more than one young
girl, when she passed by the Cherche-Midi
prison, her heart beat for the man who was
shut within.   But there was little reason in
these feelings, and Annette had not been
able to bring herself to a critical examination of the Affair.   Politics repelled her;
when she had attempted to study them at
close range, she had immediately been
turned aside by a mixture of boredom and
repugnance which she did not seek to
analyse.   Her viewpoint was too honest not
to have glimpsed the amount of pettiness
and malpractise that was shared almost
equally by both sides.   Less sincere than
her eyes, her heart wished to continue to
believe that the party which upheld ideas

of justice must be composed of the justest
men. And she reproached herself for what
she called her laziness in not becoming better acquainted with their activities. That
is why she made herself maintain an attitude of sympathetic waiting towards them,
—as when hearing the execution of a page
of new music that is guaranteed by an accepted name, a respectful listener, who does
not understand it, gives credit to beauties
that he will discover later, perhaps. . . .

Annette, being loyal, believed in the virtue of labels, ignorant of the fact that the
fraud is nowhere more current than in the
commerce of ideas. She still attributed
some reality to the fabricated *isms*, whose
stamp distinguishes the various political
faiths; and she was attracted by those proclaimed by the advanced parties. A secret
illusion made her hope that it was on this
side that she had the best chance of meeting
her mate. Accustomed to the open air, she
went in the direction of those who sought
it, like herself, outside the old prejudices,
ancient follies, and suffocation of the house
of the past. She spoke no evil of the old

dwelling. It had sheltered the lives and dreams of generations. But the air was vitiated. Remain there who would! One must breathe. And her eyes sought the friend who would help her construct her own house, sanely and clear-sightedly.

In the drawing-rooms that she frequented there was no lack of young men quite capable, it seemed, of understanding and aiding her. With or without labels, many had daring minds. But an evil fate willed that their daring should not be directed towards the same horizons as hers. In the words of the philosopher, the *elan vital* is limited. It never exercises itself, simultaneously, in all directions. Infinitely rare are the spirits that throw their light all around them as they walk. The majority of those who have succeeded in lighting their lanterns (and they are not numerous!) focus their searchlights straight ahead, upon one point, a single point; and around them they do not see a speck. One may even say that an advance in one direction is almost always paid for by a retreat in another. Many a one who is a revolutionary

in politics is an imitative conservative in art.
And if he is deprived of a handful of his
prejudices (those that he values least) he
will only clasp the others more avariciously
to his breast.

Nowhere is the unevenness of this jolt-
ing march more clearly visible than in the
moral evolution of the two sexes. The
woman who forces herself to break with
the errors of the past and who enters upon
one of the paths leading to the new society
rarely ever encounters the man who also
wishes to found a new world. He takes
another route. And if their climbing paths.
must finally, perhaps, come together further up the slope, for the moment they turn
their backs upon each other. This diver-
gence of aims was particularly striking in
France at this period, when the feminine
mind, so much longer held back, had been
making, for some years, a sudden advance,
of which the men of that day took no account. The women themselves did not
always measure it accurately, until there
came the day when the shock of personal

experience revealed to them the wall that separated them from their mates. The shock was rude. Annette, to her own cost, had to discover this unhappy misunderstanding.

VI

From among the drifting souls that swarmed about her, Annette's eyes, her distrait eyes that unsuspectedly surveyed them all, had finally made their choice. But they had not admitted it. As long as possible she tried to preserve the illusion of continued hesitation. When one no longer needs to make a decision, then it is sweet to murmur to oneself, "I am not bound as yet," and to leave the doors of hope wide open for the last time.

There were two in particular between whom she liked to leave her future in the balance, although she knew perfectly well which one she had chosen; two young men between twenty-eight and thirty: Marcel Franck and Roger Brissot. Both belonged to the comfortably situated middle class, and were distinguished in manner, pleasant and intelligent, but possessed of minds and characters of different orders.

Marcel Franck, of a half-Jewish family, was one of those charming types that are

sometimes produced by the mixed marriage
of well chosen individuals of two races.
Of medium height, slim, graceful and elegant, he had blue eyes set in a dead white
face, a slightly curved nose, a small fair
beard, and an elongated, somewhat horsey
profile that recalled Alfred de Musset. His
glance was intelligent and caressing, by
turns coaxing and impudent. His father,
a rich cloth merchant, cautious in business
and strong in his passions, who had a taste
for the new art, patronized the young re-
views, bought Van Goghs and Rousseaus,
had married a beautiful Toulousaine, who
had won the second prize in comedy at the
Conservatory, and who for a time had been
the rage at Antoine's and Porel's. This
lady, first taken by assault, and thereafter
in lawful wedlock, by the vigorous Jonas
Franck, had abandoned the stage in the
midst of her success, to maintain intelli-
gently, along with her husband's affairs, a
literary salon much frequented by artists.
This most united household, neither member of which, by tacit accord, looked too
closely into the other's conduct, and each

of whom knew how to handle gossip, had
brought up a single son in an atmosphere
of tolerant and sharpened intelligence. At
home Marcel Franck had learned that there
is a harmony of work and pleasure, and
that the art of life depends upon their wise
union. He cultivated this art no less than
the others, in which he had become a dis-
cerning connoisseur. Attracted to the national museums he had made a precocious
reputation as a writer on art. Quite as
well as pictures, he knew how to observe
living figures with his idle, penetrating, insolent, indulgent glance. And among the
young men who were courting Annette, it
was he who read her best. She was quite
aware of it. Sometimes as she was emerg-
ing from one of those absent-minded reveries, during a conversation in which she
was following every other thought but the
one she was uttering, she would meet his
curious eyes that seemed to say to her:

"Annette, I see you naked."

And the most astonishing thing was that
she, the modest Annette, was not embarrassed by this. She felt like replying:

"And how do you find me, that way?"

They exchanged an understanding smile. If he saw her unveiled, it was of slight importance; she knew that she would never be his. Marcel read this certainty in her. He was not troubled by it. He was thinking:

"We shall see about that!"

For he knew *the other*.

The other, Roger Brissot, had been a college chum of his. Franck perfectly understood that Annette preferred him. . . . To begin with, at least . . . ("Afterward? . . . That is another affair! . . .") Brissot was a handsome fellow, with a fine open countenance, a frank expression, gay brown eyes, regular features that were rather strong, a full face, sound teeth,—cleanshaven, with a youthful abundance of black hair combed back from an intelligent brow and parted at the side. Tall, broad-chested, long of leg, and with well-muscled arms, his movements were easy and his actions lively. He spoke well, very well, in a warm musical voice, a little low and resonant, that people liked,—that he liked.

With his quick, ready, glittering intelligence, he rivaled Franck in his studies, and was no less fond of athletics. In Burgundy, where his family's property—woods and vineyards—adjoined the Rivière's country place, he was an intrepid walker, hunter, and horseman. In the old days Annette had met him more than once on his walks. But at that time she had given scant thought to a companion, she liked to go her own way; and Roger too, having slipped away from Paris for these months in the open air, played the young Hippolyte, affecting to prefer his horse and his dog to a girl. In passing, they had exchanged no more than bows and glances. But those had not been entirely lost. Agreeable images remained, and the vague attraction of two beings physically well suited.

The idea had occurred to the Brissot family. No less than their persons, their fortunes seemed made for union. However, so long as Raoul Rivière lived, the neighborly relations had remained polite enough, but rather cold and distant. By a

curious freak, Rivière, who would have
yielded to no man as a free thinker, had
as an architect numbered his clients, until
the Dreyfus Affair, almost exclusively in
the aristocracy and the reactionary camp;
and as he was too clever not to give them
lip service, and even to go to mass when
it was useful that he should be noticed, he
passed for a reactionary and even a clerical
(which made him laugh heartily!) in the
eyes of the radical republicans of his province.   Now the Brissots were pillars of
radicalism.   This family of the robe—ad-
vocates and attorneys—who prided themselves on having been republicans for more
than a century (their republicanism dated,
indeed, from the days of the First Republic, but they forgot to mention that their
ancestor had received the Order of the Lily
upon the return of the Bourbons), believed
in the Republic as others believe in God
the Father, and they considered themselves
bound by their traditions: *noblesse oblige!*
So the Brissots had felt it was their duty
to manifest their austere censure of Raoul
Rivière by holding him at a distance; which

did not bother him at all, as he expected
no commissions from them. Came the
famous Dreyfus Affair, in which Rivière,
as we have seen, found himself, without
dreaming of such a thing, in the Pro-
gressive party. In a flash, he was white-
washed; a sponge was applied to his past,
and people even discovered in Rivière
exalted civic and republican virtues, which
he himself would never have suspected, but
from which he would assuredly have de-
rived excellent profit, had death not come
to spoil his plans.

The Brissots' plans had not suffered in
consequence. These great republicans who,
for a century, had known boldly how to harmonize their principles and their interests,
were rich; and, naturally, they dreamed of
being more so. They knew that Rivière
had left his daughter a very tidy fortune.
It would be very nice to unite his Burgundy property to the Brissot possessions,
which it would complete so happily. But
with people who had such principles as the
Brissots, worldly reasons came second,—
even when it happened that they thought

of them first: in a question of marriage, it
was the young girl who must first be taken
into account. The young girl, in this in-
stance, answered all requirements. Annette
satisfied them by what they knew of her,
by her serious ways, and by what they had
learned of her devotion to her father.
They were impressed by her intelligence
and by her simplicity. Her bearing in
society was perfect. She had composure.
Enough wit. Good health. Doubtless her
work at the Sorbonne, her studies and her
diplomas, seemed a little affected to them;
but they considered these the pastimes of
an intelligent young girl who was bored,
and who would put them aside when her
first child arrived. And the Brissots were
not averse to showing that they liked intelligence, even in a woman,—provided,
naturally, it did not become embarrassing.
Annette would not be the first feminine
intellectual in the family, thank Heaven!
Madame Brissot, the mother, and Roger's
sister Adèle, enjoyed the reputation, justified in a sense, of being brainy women, no
less than women of sentiment, who were

able to share the mental life as well as the active life of the men of their household. Annette's intellectuality was at least a guarantee (the great point!) that in her case there was no danger of clericalism. For the rest, she would find in her new family affectionate guidance that would know how to guard her from any extravagances. It would not be difficult for the dear child to become part of the family whose name she was to take: she had no parents, and she would be only too glad to put herself under the ægis of a second mother and a slightly older sister, who would ask merely to guide her. For the Brissot ladies, who were keen observers, judged Annette to be really congenial, very distinguished, sweet, polished, reserved, timid (from their point of view this was not a fault) and a little cold (this was almost a virtue).

It was then with the support of his whole family, previously consulted, that Roger paid his court. He hid nothing from them, sure that he would always meet with approval. This big fellow was idolized by his family, and he repaid them in

full measure. The Brissots practiced mutual admiration. There was a hierarchy,
but each had his worth. It had to be recognized that they were all fairly evenly
endowed on the mental side, as well as with
the advantages of body and of fortune.
They recognized the fact, but gracefully,
like well-bred people. They never showed
it to those whom they considered plainly
their inferiors. But the truth could not be
doubted, from the sweet certainty written
on their features. Of all their certainties,
Roger was the most certain. He was their
dearest pride, and perhaps the best justified. Never had the Brissot tree borne
more thriving fruit. Roger had the best
gifts of his race, and if he had its faults
as well, they were not startling: his charm
and his youth caused them to be forgotten.
He was full of talent, all things were easy
for him, but especially speech. Eloquence
was one of the family fiefs. It already
counted one barrister; and from birth all
the Brissots had a love of fine speech. It
would have been an injustice to pretend
that, like those talkers of the Midi, they

had to talk in order to think; but they had to talk,—that was incontestable. Their real faculties bloomed in phrases; silence would have atrophied them. Roger's father, one of the most illustrious gabblers that ever honored the tribune of the Chamber, and on whom the voters had played the scurvy trick of not reelecting him, was suffocated by his stifled eloquence; and Roger, then aged six, used to say to him naïvely when they were alone by the hearth:

"Papa, make me a speech!"

Now he made them on his own account. In a trice his youthful reputation had been brilliantly established at the legal conferences at the Palais-Bourbon. Like all the Brissots, he had turned his gifts towards politics. The meetings in connection with the Dreyfus Affair had furnished him with an excellent springboard; he bounded into the arena, delivering speeches in mid-flight. The youthful fire, bravura, and well chosen, overflowing speech of this handsome young man, won for him the enthusiastic sympathy of the young feminine

Dreyfusistes and many of his juniors. The Brissots, ever desirous of not allowing themselves to be outdistanced on the road of Progress, but very careful not to go a step too far or too early, having carefully surveyed the terrain, spurred their son, their young pride, along the way of serious socialism. Roger, his nose to the trail, gave himself to the task. Like the flower of the youth of his day, he was under the spell of Jaurès, and he tried to model his orations on the splendid speeches of the great rhetorician, filled with prophetic visions and illusory mirages. He proclaimed the necessity of an understanding between the people and the intellectuals. This furnished him a theme for the most eloquent speeches. Even though the people—who lacked leisure—did not know much about it, they were seriously disturbing the leisure of the young bourgeoisie. With personal subscriptions and the assistance of a small group of friends, Roger founded a study club, a newspaper, a party. He spent a great deal of time and a little money on them. The Brissots, who were good reckoners, also knew how to spend on occasion. They were pleased to see their son become a leader of the younger generation. They prepared the ground for the coming elections. Roger was marked for a place in the future Chamber. Nor was he ignorant of the fact. Accustomed from childhood to see his family believe in him, he believed in himself, too; and without precisely knowing what his ideas were, he had an absolute faith in them. In no way overweening. He was full of himself, but so naturally! He was successful in everything; he was so accustomed to it that it did not even occur to him to pride himself on the fact; but he would have been dumbfounded had it been otherwise, his surest dogmas would have received a serious blow. How likable he was! A naïve, unconscious and shallow egotist, a good fellow and a handsome fellow, disposed to give but determined to receive, and unable to conceive that anything could be refused him, simple, polite, cordial, demanding, waiting for the world to place itself at his feet. . . . He was really very attractive.

VII

Annette felt the attraction. She judged him accurately enough, but this only made her love him the more. She smiled at his foibles, which were infinitely dear to her. These made him seem to her less the man, and more the child; and her heart rejoiced that he was one as well as the other. One of Roger's charms was that he hid nothing; he showed his entire self. His innocent satisfaction with himself gave him a perfect naturalness.

He was all the more confiding because he was enamoured of Annette. Ardently and without reservations. He loved nothing by halves. But he never saw more than half of anything.

His fire for her was kindled one evening when he had been very eloquent in some drawing-room. Annette had said nothing, but she had listened marvelously. (At least he thought so.) Her intelligent eyes returned his own thoughts to him, clearer

and more winged. Her smile gave him
joy in what he had said so well, and it was
all the sweeter because he felt that it was
shared. . . . How beautiful she was, that
listening girl! What an admirable mind,
what an exceptional soul, could be discerned
in those attentive, speaking eyes, in that
all-understanding smile! . . . Although he
was the only one to speak, he had the illusion that he was talking with her. In any
case, he no longer spoke save for her; and
he felt himself being lifted above himself
by this inward dialogue, by the mysterious
exchange of these mute responses. . . .

As a matter of fact, Annette was scarcely
listening. Sufficiently intelligent to seize
promptly the general drift of Roger's
thought, she followed absentmindedly, as
was her habit, the fine balanced phrases.
But she profited by his absorption in his
eloquence to study him thoroughly: eyes,
mouth and hands, the way he moved his
chin when he talked, his fine nostrils resem-
bling those of a neighing colt, his habit of
prettily rolling certain letters, and all that
this expressed, both inside and out. . . .

She could see into him. She perceived his desire to be admired, she saw the pleasure that he took in pleasing, and she judged him handsome, intelligent, eloquent, amazing. And it did not occur to her at all (yes! a little, a very little . . .) to find him comical. On the contrary, she found him very touching. . . .

. . . "Yes, my dear, you are handsome, you are charming, intelligent, eloquent, amazing. . . . You want a little smile? . . . There, my dear, I give you two . . . with my very sweetest eyes. . . . Are you satisfied? . . .")

In her heart she laughed, when she saw him, all happiness and pride, redouble his warbling like a spring bird.

Homage was sweet to him; he drank it undiluted, without a drop of irony; he wanted more, he was never wearied. And, intoxicated by his own song, he could no longer distinguish it from the person who admired it. She seemed to him the incarnation of all that was beautiful, pure and genial in it. He adored her.

She, into whose heart love had glided at

first sight,—when she felt herself bathed
in this adoration, no longer offered the least
resistance. Even the gentle irony that, like
a gorget, protected the beatings of her
heart, fell from her; and she offered her
bare breast to love. She was so hungry for
affection! What happiness to slake her
thirst (she anticipated the joy) at the lips
of this man who charmed her! How he
offered them to her, anticipating her desire,
with such a burst of ardor, permeating her
with a passionate gratitude. . . .

The fire was well ablaze. Each burned
with the other's desire, and fed upon his
own. And the more the one was exalted,
the more he expected of the other; and
the more the other strove to surpass that
expectation. It was very tiring, but they
had an immense youthful energy to
spend.

For the moment, Annette's energy was
reduced to a passive rôle. None other was
left her. Roger invaded her. She was
submerged. He scarcely gave her time to
breathe. His expansive, overflowing nature
felt the need of telling all, of confiding

all: future, past and present. And it was
long! But Roger held his ground! He
also wanted to know all, to have all. He
forcibly penetrated Annette's secrets. Annette was hard pressed to defend her last
retreats. A little scandalized, happy and
amused, she had a faint desire to fly into a
passion at this invasion; but the invader was
so adorable! . . . She abandoned herself,
voluptuously; she experienced, in yielding to
this mental rape,—(*Et cognovit eam. . . .*"
He scarcely knew her! . . .)—secret feelings of revolt and pleasure. . . .

It was not over-prudent, this complete
surrender of self. There was the risk that
certain confidences, made in hours of abandon, might later be employed as weapons
by the confidant. But this was the very
least of Annette's and Roger's cares. At
this hour of love, nothing in the beloved
could displease, nothing could astonish. All
that the loved one confided, far from sur-
prising the lover, seemed a response to his
own unuttered vows. Roger no longer
guarded—guarded less than ever—the in-
discreet confessions that Annette's indulgent

ear was none the less registering very faithfully, unknown to him.

What pleasure they took in sharing the past and the present; the present and the past were linked together in the dream of the future, of *their* future: for although Annette had said nothing, promised nothing, her acceptance was so taken for granted, so anticipated, and so demanded, that Annette herself ended by believing she had given it. Happily, with eyes half closed, she listened to Roger set forth with tireless enthusiasm the magnificent life of thought and action that was reserved for him (for he was one of those who always enjoy to-morrow more than to-day). . . . For whom? For him? For Roger. And for her too, of course, since she was a part of Roger. She was not shocked by this absorption; she was too busy seeing, hearing, drinking in, this marvellous Roger. He talked a great deal of socialism, of justice, of love, of emancipated humanity. He was really splendid. In words, his generosity knew no bounds. Annette was stirred. It was intoxicating to think that she might be associated with this work of powerful benevolence. Roger never asked her what she thought about it. It was understood that she thought as he did. She could not think otherwise. He spoke for her. He spoke for both of them, because he was the better speaker. He said:

"We shall do. . . . We shall have. . . ."

And she did not protest. On the contrary she was grateful. All this was so big, so vague, so disinterested, that she had no reason to be disturbed by it. Roger was all light and liberty. . . . A little diffuse perhaps. Annette, maybe, would have liked a little more precision. But that would come later; one couldn't say everything at once. Let us make the pleasure last! . . . To-day we have only to enjoy these limitless horizons.

She took particular joy in his charming countenance, in the ardent attraction of their two loving bodies, through which electric waves suddenly passed, in the tide of physical vigor that filled them both,— both rich in the endowment of a youth that was chaste, healthy, robust, and aflame.

Never was Roger's eloquence more certain than when it halted and, in the last vibrations of the words that had opened exalted vistas to them, their eyes met: the sudden contact was like a physical embrace. Then such desire flamed in them that their breathing stopped. Roger thought no more of dazzling and talking. Annette no longer thought of the future of humanity, nor even of her own. They forgot everything, everything about them: the drawing-room, the public. In these instants they became but a single being, a wax in the flame. Nothing more than the Desire of nature, —unique, devouring, and pure like fire. Then Annette, with distraught eyes and flaming cheeks, would wrench herself out of the vertigo, with the trembling and intoxicating certainty that some day she would succumb. . . .

VIII

Their love was no longer a secret to anyone. They were both incapable of veiling
it. Annette held her tongue in vain; her
eyes spoke for her. Their mute acquies-
cence was so eloquent that in the eyes of
the world, as in Roger's, she appeared
tacitly engaged.

The Brissot family alone did not lose
sight of the fact that she was not. To
Roger's declarations, Annette doubtless lent
herself with an evident pleasure. But she
avoided answering; she was clever enough
to turn the conversation to some great subject, on which the innocent Roger, leaving
the prey for the shadow, launched himself
endlessly, only too happy to talk. And,
once again, Annette had not spoken. Having observed this manœuver several times,
the Brissots, prudent folk that they were,
decided to take a hand. It was not that
they could harbor a doubt regarding Annette's decision and the happiness that so

brilliant a match would bring her; but, after all, one must always reckon with the strange caprices of a young girl! They knew life. They knew its pitfalls. They were crafty French provincials. When the decision that they awaited was delayed on the way, prudence counseled them to go in search of it. The two Brissot ladies took the road.

There was a smile that was known in Paris, in the circle of their acquaintances, as the Brissot smile: it was unctuous and sweet, affable and superior, measuredly and heavily playful, foreseeing all, gushing with benevolence, perfectly indifferent; it offered full hands, but the hands remained full. It adorned the two Brissot ladies.

Madame Brissot, the mother, a large handsome woman, with a broad face, fat cheeks, well-fed and chubby, had an imposing carriage, an opulent bosom, and an unctuous, excessively flattering way of talking that embarrassed the sincere Annette. But it was not meant for her alone (she soon noticed this with relief). This laudatory tone was generously distributed to all.

It was accompanied by a perpetual badinage, which with the Brissots was a courteous mark of the certainty which was intuitive with them, and of the geniality with which they recognized this superiority.

Mademoiselle Brissot, Roger's sister, also big and strong, was a very pale blond, so lacking in color that she seemed almost an albino. She accentuated this by a cloud of rice powder on her cheeks and a streak of red on her lips. She was aiming at the ideal of a Louis XV pastel. She might have served Nattier as a mincing, chlorotic, and fleshy Burgundian Phœbe. Her mother called this robust girl, "My poor little darling," for Mademoiselle Brissot, who functioned like a charm, had conceived the idea, while admiring her pallor, that her health must be delicate. But she did not exploit it by demanding coddling; on the contrary she used it to show off her energy and give herself the right to scorn the softer creatures of her sex who moaned about their little ailments. In truth, she was admirable, active, and indefatigable; she read everything, saw everything, knew

everything; she painted, was a judge of
music, talked literature; and every day, in
company with Madame Brissot, she carried
out a program of some two or three hundred calls that had to be made in a given .
time, receiving them in return, giving
dinners, following the concerts and the
theatres, the sittings of the Chamber and
the exhibitions, without ever flinching,
without ever betraying fatigue, save at
chosen moments by a bravely stifled sigh;
—and, besides all this, she knew how to
feed the body that she mortified, eating
heavily like all her family, and getting a
full night's dreamless sleep. She was no
less mistress of her heart than of her body.
She was sedately preparing for her marriage to a politician of some forty years,
who was at this moment governor of one
of the great oversea colonies. She had
not dreamed of accompanying him there.
She did not wish to leave Paris and the
Brissot name behind her until the happy
elect could offer her a position in France
that was worthy of her. In addition to
which, she knew how to keep him from

being forgotten in high places. With regularity. they wrote each other letters that were cordial and businesslike. This long-distance courtship had gone on for a number of years. Marriage would come in due time. She was in no hurry. Her husband would be rather mature, but according to Mademoiselle Brissot's taste he would be all the better for that. She had a strong head. Head, the Brissots had never lacked. Mademoiselle Brissot's was eminently political. Her mother said that she was, by vocation, an Egeria. Madame Brissot admired the intelligence of Mademoiselle Brissot. Mademoiselle Brissot admired the domestic genius and mind of Madame Brissot. They paid each other mincing compliments. They kissed each other in the presence of Annette. It was charming.

However, they soft-pedaled this mutual cult in order to cajole Annette. They were all compliments, for her, for her house, for her clothes, her taste, her wit, her beauty. The excessively laudatory tone grated on Annette a bit; but one does not remain in-

sensible to the flattering opinion that others
have of one, particularly when those others
seem messengers from the person whom one
loves. It was hard not to believe that this
was the case; for the Brissot ladies continually brought Roger's name into the
conversation. They intertwined his praises
with Annette's; they made smiling, per-
sistent allusions to the impression Annette
had produced on him, to the things she had
said to him, and which he had hastened to
repeat enthusiastically—(he repeated everything: Annette was embarrassed but none
the less touched). They laid great stress
upon his brilliant future; and Madame
Brissot assumed an impressive tone in which
to phrase her hope that Roger would find
—that he had found—a helpmate worthy
of him. She named no one, but the meaning was clear. All these little ruses were
visible to the naked eye, at twenty paces.
They were meant to be. It was a sort of
social game, in which one must talk around
the word that everyone has on his tongue,
without ever pronouncing it. Madame
Brissot's smile seemed watching Annette's

lips for the word that was about to come out, as though to cry:

"A bargain!"

Annette smiled, opened her mouth. But the word did not come. . . .

Annette was invited by the Brissots to intimate evening parties in their apartment on the Rue de Provence. She became acquainted with father Brissot, tall and big and rubicund, with cunning eyes beneath bushy brows, a short gray beard, and the air of a crafty and fatherly lawyer, who heaped upon her gallantries and ancient jests. He too tried to play the social game, but he put his foot in it with his circumlocutions. Annette took fright, and Madame Brissot signalled her husband to keep out of the affair. So he stayed outside the game, content to jeer and follow it from the corner of his eye, convinced that it was not his business and that the women would acquit themselves better than he.

With Annette, Madame Brissot at first adroitly invited only three or four intimate friends,—then two, then one, then none. And Annette found herself alone with the

four Brissots. *En famille*, said Madame
Brissot in a tone rich in unctuously maternal promises. Annette smelled the trap,
but she did not steal away. She found
too much pleasure in being with Roger.
Her affection for him made her regard his
family indulgently; she closed her eyes to
what secretly irritated her in this circle.
Acuteness of feminine instinct warned the
Mesdames Brissot of this; strong as their
self-love was, it never worked against their
interests; by tacit accord, they knew how
to efface themselves, how to speak less, sift
their ideas, and arrange matters so that the
lovers might frequently enjoy undisturbed
times alone together. More and more
enamoured and disturbed at Annette's reserve, which would have struck him less
forcibly had not his mother and his sister
called it to his attention, Roger had never
been more attracted than now when his
self-confidence was threatened. He deliv-
ered no more speeches; his eloquence had
flagged. For the first time in his life, he
tried to read another's soul. As he sat
beside Annette, his humble and ardent eyes

devoured, implored the little enigma, striving to solve it. Annette enjoyed this disquiet, this timidity that was so new in him, this fearful waiting that watched over her every movement. She was shaken. There were moments when she nearly bent towards him, to utter decisive words. And yet she did not say them. At the last second, she instinctively drew back, without knowing why; brusquely she avoided the declaration that Roger was about to make, and her own avowals. She escaped. . . .

And then the trap closed. From one of the neighboring salons, Madame and Mademoiselle Brissot would discreetly brood over the unfruitful interview. Occasionally they were visible, crossing the drawing-room, smiling and preoccupied. In passing they would throw out a friendly word, but they did not stop. And the two young people continued their long conversations.

One evening when they were absent-mindedly thumbing an album, which was an excuse for them to put their heads close together, while they were exchanging their thoughts in a low voice, there was a silence;

and suddenly Annette perceived the danger. She wanted to get up, but Roger's arm was already around her waist, and the young man's passionate mouth was upon her half-parted lips. She tried to defend herself. But how could she, against herself! Her lips returned the kiss, even while she wanted to draw away. She disengaged herself, however, when she heard Madame Brissot shrilling in an excited voice, from the other end of the drawing-room:

"Oh! my dear girl! . . ."

And she was calling:

"Adèle! . . . Monsieur Brissot! . . ."

Annette in stupefaction saw herself surrounded in a flash by the entire Brissot family, radiant and affectionate. Madame Brissot covered her with kisses, while she sponged her own eyes with a handkerchief and kept repeating:

"Love him well!"

Mademoiselle Brissot was saying:

"My little sister!"

And Monsieur Brissot, always a blunderer:

"At last! . . . You've taken long enough! . . ."

Meanwhile Roger was kneeling before Annette, kissing her hands and begging her with eyes that were fearful and a little shamefaced, asking forgiveness and imploring:

"Don't say no!"

Annette, petrified, yielded to his kisses; the supplication of those beloved eyes forged the last link in her chains. She made a final effort to protest:

("Why, I haven't said anything! . . .")

But she saw in Roger's eyes a grief so sincere that she could not bear it; and when Roger's face lighted up with happiness, her own became radiant at the joy she had caused. She clasped his head between her hands. Roger rose, crying out in relief. And, beneath the benevolent eyes of his family, they exchanged their kiss of betrothal.

IX

That night, when Annette found herself alone in her own home, she was thunder-struck. She no longer belonged to herself. She had given herself. . . . Given! Given her life! . . . Her heart contracted in anguish.

She still exaggerated the tightness of the bonds that she had just accepted. She was not one of those young girls who jest lightly with their fiancés regarding the possibility of divorce. She did not give with one hand to take back with the other. She was no longer her own. She belonged to the Brissots. And suddenly the Brissots appeared inimical. All that her eyes had seen during these past weeks came before her, with accentuated outlines: all their manœuvres of approach in order to envelop her, their conspiracy against her freedom, the final comedy that had extorted her consent by surprise. . . . (Had not Roger, Roger himself, been an accomplice? . . .) And she

bristled like a cornered animal that sees the
circle close around him, feels himself lost,
and is ready to charge with lowered head
against the hunters, either to clear a passage or to die and win vengeance. For the
first time, everything in the Brissots that
displeased her, thoughts of which she had
hitherto avoided, appeared to her magni-
fied, hateful, and intolerable. . . . Even
Roger! . . . Never could she live im-
mured in that man, that family, that circle
of interests which were not her own, which
never could be. She decided to break
away. . . .

But could she still break away, now that
she had just become engaged? Would
Roger permit it? He would have to permit it! He couldn't prevent her. . . . At
the idea that he might oppose it, Annette
hated him. In that moment, the other's
suffering did not count, she would not have
hesitated to break his heart in order to
recover her own liberty. . . . And then she
remembered his imploring eyes. . . . And
she was overawed. . . . No matter! The
egotism of menaced life, the instinct of

self-preservation were stronger than all else, stronger than tenderness, stronger than pity! She had to save herself. And woe to him who barred her escape! . . .

All night long, twisting and turning in her bed, devoured by a feverish insomnia, she lived through in anticipation the scene that she was going to have with Roger. She repeated, tried out all the words that he and she would utter. She tried to convince him, she argued, she flew into a passion, she pled with him, and she detested him. Dawn found her exhausted but decided. She would go to Roger's house. . . . Or, no! she would write to him; in that way she would be freer to finish what she had to say without interruption. She would break it off. To avoid the Brissots returning to the charge, she resolved to leave Paris, to spend a few days at some hotel in the suburbs. And getting up, she wrote her letter, the phrases of which she had rehearsed in her head a hundred times. Then she hastily began her preparations for departure.

She was in the midst of them when

Roger surprised her at it. She had not thought of barring her door, as it had not occurred to her that he might come so early. He entered, preceding in his amorous impatience the servant who announced him. He was bringing flowers. He was bubbling over with happiness and gratitude. He was so affectionate, so young, so charming that when Annette saw him she no longer had the strength to speak. All her fine resolutions were forgotten, her heart was recaptured at the first glance. With the astonishing bad faith of love, she immediately found as many reasons for marriage as she had found against it a moment before. She tried to fight, but joy shone in her eyes, ringed by the worries of the night. She looked at her Roger, who was drinking her in with an intoxicated glance, and she said to herself:

"But I have decided . . . but I must decide. . . . What is it I have decided? . . ."

But how could she know, when he looked at her as though he were drinking in her very soul! Think, how could she think, how recover herself! . . . She no longer knew, she was lost. . . . And, meanwhile, it was so good to feel that she was loved! All that she could do, with an immense effort, was to ask Roger not to hasten the marriage. And immediately Roger looked so disappointed, so cast down, that Annette had not the courage to go on. How could she hurt so dear a boy? She hastened tenderly to reassure him, to tell him that she loved him; feebly she tried to cling to her postponement, which he repulsed as energetically as though it were a matter of life and death. Finally, after a loving bargaining on both sides, they agreed to compromise; and their marriage was fixed for the middle of the summer.

Afterwards, Roger left; and Annette, regarding herself sheepishly in the mirror, found there all her indecision again. . . . How could she get out of it? She contemplated the interrupted preparations for her journey.

"Well done!" said she.

She shrugged her shoulders, laughed. . . . How charming Roger was! . . . Back into the closet went her lingerie and the things she had taken out for her trunk. . . .

"But just the same," she was thinking, "I don't want to, I don't want to! . . ."

Nervously she let fall a pile of chemisettes. . . . Thump! And toilet brushes went tumbling after. . . . Impatiently she kicked the heap. . . .

And then she gathered them up, bending down to the floor. In the midst of her tidying, she let herself go and sat down on the parquet, not very proud of her will power. . . .

"Nonsense!" she exclaimed, stretching herself out on the carpet, "I still have four months to change my mind. . . ."

And with her face thrust into a cushion, lying flat on her stomach, she counted the days. . . .

X

The Brissots prudently gave their approval of Annette's expressed desire to prolong the engagement: they did not wish to imperil their success by showing too much haste. But they felt it necessary to surround Annette during these months of waiting. It would not do to leave her to herself; there was always a risk of the strange girl escaping.

Easter Sunday was approaching. The Brissots invited Annette to spend Easter week with them at their country place in Burgundy. Annette accepted regretfully; she was tempted and afraid; afraid of adding to the chains that already bound her, afraid of being completely captured or of breaking everything; and afraid of still other things, more dangerous, that she did not like to consider. She did not wish to escape from the state of amorous uncertainty in which she was allowing herself to be cradled: she suffered from it a little, and

246

she found a certain charm in it. She would
have liked to prolong it. But she knew
perfectly well that it was not wholesome,
and that she had not the right to do so,
face to face with Roger.

Finally she decided to lay her troubles
before Sylvie. Never had she said a word
to her of her love for Roger. Yet she confided everything to her: of all the other
young men she had often spoken to her.
. . . Yes, but she didn't love the other
young men! And Roger's name had been
kept out of their conversation.

Sylvie exclaimed, called her "Sneak!"
and laughed uproariously when Annette
tried to explain her indecision, her scruples
and her torments.

"Well now," she demanded, "is this bird
of yours handsome?"

"Yes," replied Annette.

"He loves you?"

"Yes."

"And you love him?"

"I love him."

"Well then, what's stopping you?"

"Oh! it is so difficult! How can I tell

you? . . . I love him. . . . I love him tremendously. . . . He is so wonderful!"

(She began to describe him complaisantly, under Sylvie's mocking eyes. Then she broke off. . . .)

"I love him very much . . . very much. . . . And then, too, I don't love him. . . . There are things about him . . . I could never live with . . . I never could. . . . And then, he loves me too much. He would like to eat me. . . ."

(Sylvie burst out laughing.)

". . . It's true, eat me entirely, devour my whole life, all my own thoughts, the very air I breathe. . . . Oh! he's an excellent eater, my Roger! It's a pleasure to see him at the table. . . . He has a good appetite. . . . But I, I don't want to be eaten."

She too laughed heartily; and Sylvie, who was sitting in her lap, laughed against her neck. Annette went on:

"It's frightful to feel yourself being devoured like that, alive, to have nothing of your own any more, not to be able to keep anything any longer. . . . And he doesn't suspect it. . . . He loves me madly, and I have an idea, you see, that he doesn't even try to understand me, that he doesn't even think about it. He comes, he takes, he carries me off. . . ."

"Well, that's terribly nice!" observed Sylvie.

"You are always thinking about silly things!" said Annette, clasping her in her arms.

"And what would you like to have me think about?"

"About marriage. That's a serious thing."

"Serious! oh! well, not so serious!"

"What, it isn't serious to give all of yourself, without a single reservation?"

"And who talked about doing that? You'd have to be mad!"

"But he wants to have everything!"

Sylvie squirmed with laughter like a little fish.

"Oh! you goose! you stupid! . . . Ninny!"

(It seemed to her so simple to say what one wished, to give what one wished, and to keep back all the rest without saying anything about it! She was affectionately ironical towards men and their demands. They are not so sharp! . . .)

"But I'm not, I'm not all those things," Annette protested.

"Oh! So far as that goes!" exclaimed Sylvie, "you take everything so seriously."

Annette admitted the fact, contritely.

"It's too bad all the same! . . . I wish I were like you! . . . You have all the luck!" she went on.

"Let's exchange! Hand over yours!" said Sylvie.

Annette had no desire to exchange. Sylvie left her comforted.

But at the same time, Annette did not understand herself. She was puzzled.

"It's curious!" she said to herself, "I want to give everything. And I want to keep everything! . . ."

The next day—it was the eve of her departure—while she was finishing her preparations, when she was beginning to torment herself again, a singular visit added to her

anxieties, at the same time clarifying them.
Marcel Franck was announced.

After a few amiably courteous speeches,
he alluded to Annette's engagement, of
which Roger had made no mystery. Gracefully he felicitated her, his voice and eyes
gently ironic, affectionate. Annette felt
very much at ease with him, as with a
perspicacious friend to whom one need not
say all, from whom one need hide nothing,—for half-words carry understanding.
They talked of Roger, whom Marcel
envied, smilingly. Annette knew that he
spoke the truth, and that he was in love.
But it caused them no perturbation. She
asked him questions about Roger, whom he
knew intimately. Marcel sang his praises;
but when she insisted that he speak of him
in a somewhat less banal fashion, he jok-
ingly said that it was useless for him to
describe Roger, as she knew him quite as
well as he. And, saying this, he fixed her
with so penetrating a glance that, for an
abashed moment, she turned away her eyes.
Then, staring in turn at him, she encountered his shrewd smile which showed that

they understood each other. They talked
for some time of indifferent matters, and
then Annette abruptly interrupted, in a
preoccupied tone:

"Tell me frankly," she said, "do you
think I've made a mistake?"

"I should never think of you as being
mistaken," said he.

"No, don't be polite! You are the one
person who can tell me the truth."

"But you know that my position is pe-
culiarly delicate."

"I know it. But I know, too, that it
has no effect on the sincerity of your judgment."

"Thanks!" said he.

She continued:

"You think that we are mistaken, Roger
and I?"

"I think that you are deceiving your-
selves."

She bowed her head. Then she said:

"I think so too."

Marcel did not respond. He continued
to look at her and smile.

"Why are you smiling?"

"I was sure that you thought so."

Annette, turning her eyes upon him, asked:

"Tell me, now, what I seem like to you?"

"I should teach you nothing."

"You will help me to see more clearly."

"You are," Marcel said to her, "an amorous rebel. Perpetually amorous (forgive me!) and perpetually rebellious. You feel the need of giving yourself, and you feel the need of withholding yourself. . . ."

(Annette could not conceal a slight start.)

"I shock you?"

"No, no, quite the contrary! How true it is! Go on! Tell me some more. . . ."

"You are," Marcel continued, "an independent who cannot remain alone. It is the law of nature. You feel it more keenly, because you are more alive."

"Yes, you understand me! You understand me better than he does. But . . ."

"But it is he whom you love."

There was no bitterness in the tone. Very friendlily they stared at each other, amused at the strangeness of human nature.

"It is not easy to live," said Annette, "to live in pairs."

"Why, yes, it would be easy enough, if men hadn't spent their time for centuries ingeniously complicating life by reciprocal restraints. The only thing to do is to throw them off. But naturally our excellent Roger, like any good old Frenchman, doesn't conceive of the idea. They think that they are lost if they no longer feel themselves weighed down by the restraints of the past. *'Where there is no restraint, there is no pleasure . . .'* especially when in being restrained one restrains one's neighbor."

"What is your conception of marriage, then?"

"As an intelligent association of interests and pleasures. Life is a vine that we exploit in common; together we cultivate it and gather the grapes. But we are not compelled always to drink our wine together, always tête-à-tête. There is a mutual complaisance that demands from and gives to the other the clusters of pleasure, of which each disposes, and which allows one discreetly to finish his harvesting elsewhere.

"What you mean," asked Annette, "is the liberty of adultery?"

"The old obsolete word! What I mean," answered Marcel, "is the liberty of love, the most essential of all liberties."

"That's the thing of least importance to me," said Annette. "For me marriage is not a public square in which one gives oneself to every passer-by. I give myself to one alone. The day on which I ceased to love and loved another, I should separate from the first; I should not divide myself between them, and I could not bear the division."

Marcel made an ironic gesture that seemed to say:

"What does it matter? . . ."

"So you see, my friend," Annette went on, "in the last analysis, I am still further away from you than from Roger."

"So you too," demanded Marcel, "belong to the good old school: 'Let us hamper one another'?"

"The one grandeur of marriage," said Annette, "is monogamous love, the fidelity of two hearts. If that is lost, what remains outside of a few practical advantages?"

"They are not negligible," said Marcel.

"They are not enough," replied Annette, "to compensate for the sacrifices."

"If that's your opinion, what are you complaining about? You rivet the bars from which one would deliver you."

"The liberty that I want," said Annette, "is not that of the heart. I feel that I am strong enough to keep that intact for the one to whom I give it."

"Are you so sure of that?" Marcel demanded tranquilly.

Annette was not so sure of it! She too was doubtful. It was her mother's daughter who was speaking at this moment, it was not the whole Annette. But she did not wish to admit it, especially to Marcel, and in an argument. She said:

"I wish it."

"Will power in such matters! . . ." exclaimed Marcel, with his shrewd smile.

". . . It is as though one decreed that a red fire should be a green fire. Love is a lighthouse of changing fires."

But Annette obstinately said:

"Not for me! . . . I don't want it to be!"

She was perfectly aware, and with the same conviction, of the need of change and of the need of permanence, those two passionate instincts of all vigorous lives. But, turn and turn about, whichever one of these two felt itself threatened, revolted.

Marcel, being well acquainted with the proud and obstinate girl, bowed politely. Annette, who judged herself as accurately as he judged her, said a little shamefacedly:

"After all, I shouldn't like . . ."

And, with this concession made to the spirit of truth, she continued more firmly, now feeling herself to be on ground of which she was sure:

"But I should like, in exchange for the gift of mutual affection, that each should preserve the right to live according to his own soul, to walk in his own way, to seek his own truth, to secure, if need be, his own

field of activity,—to carry out, in a word,
the proper law of his own spiritual life, and
not sacrifice himself to the law of another,
even the dearest person of all: for no one
has the right to immolate another's soul,
or his own for the sake of another. It is
a crime."

"That's all very fine, my dear friend,"
said Marcel, "but for me, you know, the
soul is a little beyond my depth. Perhaps
it may mean more to Roger. But I am
afraid that in that case he will not understand it in the same fashion. I can't quite
see the Brissots, in their family circle, con-
ceiving the possibility of any spiritual law
save that of the political and private fortunes of the Brissots."

"By the way," said Annette, smiling,
"to-morrow I'm going to their place in
Burgundy to spend two or three weeks."

"Well," remarked Marcel, "that will be
a case of confronting their idealism with
your own. For they are great idealists, they
too! After all, perhaps I am mistaken.
At bottom you are admirably made to get
along together."

"Don't dare me!" said Annette. "Perhaps I shall come back an accomplished
Brissot."

"Dear me! That wouldn't be so cheer-
ful! . . . No, no, I beg of you! . . .
Brissot, or not Brissot, preserve us Annette!"

"Alas! I should like to lose her, but I
can't, I'm afraid," Annette replied.

He said good-bye, kissing her hand.

"It's a pity, all the same! . . ."

He left. Annette, too, told herself that
it was a pity, but not in the same sense that
Marcel meant. It was in vain that he saw
her clearly; he understood her no more than
did Roger, who did not see her at all. To
understand her required more "religious"
souls—more religiously free—than those of
almost all these young Frenchmen. Those
who are religious, are so in the tradition of
Catholicism, which means obedience and
the renunciation of intellectual liberty
(especially in the case of a woman). And
those whose minds are free rarely suspect
the profound needs of the soul.

XI

Roger was waiting with the carriage at the little Burgundy station, where Annette arrived the following day. The instant she saw him, her cares took flight. Roger was so happy! And she was no less so. She was grateful to the Brissot ladies for having found weak excuses for not coming to meet her.

It was a clear spring evening. The golden horizon encircled the gentle undulations of pale, new grass and red, plowed land. Larks were chirping. The two-wheeled cart flew over the white road, which rang under the hoofs of the spirited little horse, and the sharp air whipped Annette's red cheeks. She sat pressed against her young companion, who, even while he drove, laughed and talked with her, and, suddenly bending over her lips, took and gave a kiss in mid-flight. She did not resist. She loved him, she loved him! But this did not prevent her realizing that she would soon begin to judge him

again, to judge herself. It is one thing to
judge, and another to love. She loved him
as she loved this air, this sky, this breath
from the fields, like a bit of spring. To-
morrow was time enough to clarify her
thoughts! To-day she gave herself a holi-
day. Let us enjoy this delicious hour! It
will not come again. . . . It seemed to her
that she was flying above the earth, with
her beloved.

They arrived only too soon, although
they went slowly at the last turning, when
they were ascending the poplar-lined road,
and even though, when they stopped to
rest the horse beneath the shadow of the
high hedges that masked the front of the
château, they embraced for a long time
without speaking.

The Brissots put their best foot forward.
They knew how to find delicate words by
which tactfully to evoke the memory of her
father. That first evening in the family
circle, Annette let herself be mothered,
grateful and touched; she had so long been
deprived of the affectionate warmth of a

home! She wanted to delude herself.
Everyone helped her to do this. Her resistance slumbered. . . .

But when she awoke in the middle of
the night, and listened to the gnawing of a
mouse in the silence of the old house, the
idea of a mouse-trap came into her mind;
and she said to herself:

"I am caught. . . ."

She felt a pang, she tried to reason with
herself.

"No, no, I don't want to be; I am
not . . ."

A nervous sweat moistened her shoulders.
She said:

"To-morrow I shall talk to Roger seriously. He must know what I am like.
We must see each other honestly if we are
going to live together. . . ."

But when the next day came, she was so
glad to see Roger again, to let herself be
enveloped in his warm affection, to breathe
with him the intoxicating sweetness of the
spring countryside, to dream of happiness
—(impossible perhaps, but who knows, who

knows? . . . perhaps it is close . . . one need only stretch out a hand . . .)—that she put off explanations until the next day. . . . And then, to the next. . . . And then, to the day after. . . .

And each night she was seized anew by piercing pangs, by heart burnings. . . .

"I must. . . . I must speak. . . . It has to be done for Roger's sake. Every day he is more enchained, and enchains me more. I have no right to keep silent. It is deceiving him. . . ."

Heavens, heavens! How weak she was! . . . Yet she was not so, in ordinary life. But the breath of love is like those hot winds whose burning languor breaks your joints and makes your heart faint. An extreme lassitude of obscure pleasure. A fear of stirring. A fear of thinking. . . . The soul, cowering in its dream, fears awakening. Annette knew perfectly well that at her first gesture the dream would be shattered. . . .

But even if we do not move, time moves for us; and the flight of days is sufficient to carry away the illusion that we would preserve. In vain one watches oneself; two persons cannot live together from morn till evening without, at the end of a short time, showing themselves as they really are.

The Brissot family revealed its true colors. The smile was façade. Annette had become part of the household. She saw busy, morose, middle-class people, who administered their wealth with a bitter pleasure. There was no question here of socialism. Of immortal principles, they invoked only the Declaration of the Landlord's Rights. It was not good to attack this. Their watchman was ceaselessly occupied in setting up barriers against trespassing. They personally exercised a strict surveillance that was to them a kind of sorry delectation. They seemed to be carrying on a guerrilla warfare with the servants, their farmers, the grape gatherers, and with all their neighbors. The spirit of sharp practice, that was native to the family and to the province, flourished here. When father Brissot succeeded in trapping someone he had his eye out for, he laughed heartily. But he did not laugh last: his adversary was made of the same Burgundian clay, not to be caught napping; the next day he retaliated by a trick of his own. And then it began all over again. . . .

Of course, Annette was not invited to participate in these ructions; the Brissots talked about them among themselves, in the drawing-room or at table, when Roger and Annette seemed occupied with each other. But Annette's keen attention followed everything that was said around her. Besides, Roger would interrupt the most loving dialogue to take part in the discussion that passionately interested them all. Then they grew heated, they all talked at once, they forgot Annette. Or they called upon her to witness facts of which she was ignorant.—Until finally, Madame Brissot, recalling the listener's presence, cut short the colloquy, and, turning her melting smile upon Annette, shifted the conversation into more flowery paths. Then, with no transition, they returned to affable good fellowship. There was in the general tone of the conversation a curious alloy of pru-

dery and frankness,—just as liberality and
stinginess were mingled in the château life.
Lively Monsieur Brissot made puns. Mademoiselle Brissot talked poetry, and on this
subject everyone had his say. They all
pretended to a knowledge of it. Their
taste dated back some twenty years. On
everything to do with art, they had fixed
opinions. They relied on the tried and true
opinions of their "friend so and so" who
belonged to the Institute and was much
decorated. No more timid minds, in the
face of authority, could be imagined than
these big bourgeois who thought that they
were as advanced in art as in politics, and
who were advanced in neither one nor the
other; for in both they never, wittingly,
arrived on the field until after the battle
had been won.

Annette felt herself far away from them.
She looked, listened, and asked herself:

"What have I to do with these people?"

The idea that one or another of them
might presume to act as her guardian did
not even repel her any more, it made her
want to laugh. She asked herself what

Sylvie would have thought, had she been blessed with a family of this sort. What shouts, what bursts of laughter! . . .

Annette answered them sometimes, when she was all alone in the garden. And it happened that Roger heard her one day, and asked in astonishment:

"What in the world is making you laugh?"

To which she replied:

"Nothing, dear. I don't know. Nonsense. . . ."

And she tried to reassume her soberest expression. But it was stronger than she: she began laughing harder than ever, even in front of the Brissot ladies. She begged pardon, and the Mesdames Brissot, indulgent and a little vexed, said:

"The child! She has to get rid of her laughter!"

But she was not always laughing. Shadows passed abruptly over her good humor. After hours of radiant tenderness and confidence with Roger, she experienced, without transition, and for no cause, attacks of melancholy, doubt, and anxiety. The instability from which her thoughts had suffered since last autumn, far from being calmed, was accentuated during these months of requited love. There came, in flurries, an invasion of strangely unharmonious instincts: irritability, grotesque humor, malignant irony, umbrageous pride, inexplicable fits of spite. Annette found it hard to put a damper on them. And the result was not so splendid, for when she did she seemed plunged in a hostile and disquieting taciturnity. As her intelligence remained clear, she was astonished at these sudden changes, and reproached herself for them. That didn't improve matters. But the realization of her own imperfections gave her a certain indulgence—more wished for than sincere—towards those of these "clowns." . . . (Again! . . . Impertinent girl! . . . Forgive me! I won't do it again! . . .) Since they were Roger's relations, she ought to accept them, if she accepted Roger. The rest, Good Heavens, the rest is of no great importance when there are two to defend each other.

Only, were there two? Would Roger

defend her?   And, even before considering
whether she would accept Roger, would
Roger accept her sincerely and with a generous heart when he finally saw what she
was like?   For up to date he had seen only
her mouth and eyes.   As regarded what
she thought and wished—the true Annette
—it did not seem that he had tried very
hard to become acquainted with her; he
found it more comfortable to invent her.
However, Annette cradled herself in the
hope that, with the aid of love, it would
not be impossible, after bravely looking into
each other's hearts, for them to say to each
other: "I take you, I take you as you are.
I take you with your faults, your demons,
with your little demands, with your law of
life.   You are what you are.   As you are,
I love you."

She knew that, for her part, she was
capable of this act of love.   During the
last days she had observed Roger at length,
with her bright eyes in which, unknown to
him, everything was mirrored.   Roger, no
long unsure of himself, had frequently
shown himself to be more of a Brissot than

she would have wished; he was obsessed by
the interests and the quarrels of his tribe,
and even brought to them the same tricky
spirit.   Certain little hard, crafty sides of
him did not please her.   But she did not
wish to judge them severely, as she would
have done in the case of others.   To her
these traits seemed imitative.   In many
things, Roger appeared to her still an uncertain child, under the thumb of his family,
whom he religiously copied, with marked
timidity of spirit, despite all his big words.
Although she began to perceive a lack of
consistency in his projects for social reform,
and although she was no longer completely duped by his eloquent idealism, she
bore him no grudge for that, for she knew
that he was not trying to deceive her, and
that he was his own first dupe; she was
even ready, with a tender irony, to remove
from his path all that might disturb the
illusion by which he had to live.   And even
his naïve egotism, which he sometimes displayed in a cumbersome fashion, did not
repel her; it seemed to her devoid of evil
intention.   At bottom, all his faults were

faults of weakness. And the amusing thing
was that he posed as strength itself. . . .
The man of bronze. . . . *Æs triplex.* . . .
Poor Roger! . . . It was almost touching.
Annette laughed very softly, but she reserved for him a wealth of indulgence.
She loved him dearly. Despite everything,
she saw him as good, generous and ardent.
She was like a mother who treats with a
gentle hand the little, and to her eyes not
very serious, vices of a dear child: she does
not hold him responsible for them, she is
only the more disposed to fuss over him and
coddle him. Ah! and then Annette had
for Roger not merely the indulgent eyes of
a mother! She had the very partial eyes
of a lover. The body was speaking; and
its voice was very strong. The voice of
reason could say what it pleased: there was
a way of hearing that made these very
faults set fire to desire. Annette saw everything clearly. But just as one may bend
one's head and squint one's eyes in order to
harmonize the planes of a landscape, so
Annette, when she looked at Roger's unpleasant traits, viewed them from an angle

that softened them. It would have not been much beyond her to love even deformities: for one gives more of oneself when one loves the faults of one's beloved; in loving what is fine, one does not give, one takes. Annette thought:

"I am glad that you are imperfect. If you knew what I see, it would annoy you. Forgive me! I have seen nothing. . . . But I, I am not like you; I want you to see me as imperfect! I am what I am, and I hold to it; my imperfections are myself, more than the rest. If you take me, you take them. Do you take them? . . . But you don't wish to know them. When will you finally take the trouble to really look at me?"

XII

Roger was in no hurry. After a few
futile attempts to lead him on to this dangerous ground from which he seemed to
flee, Annette, interrupting their conversation in the midst of a walk, stopped, took
both his hands in hers, and said:

"Roger, we must have a talk."

"Talk!" he exclaimed, laughing. "But
it doesn't seem to me that we deprive our-
selves of that!"

"No," she said, "I don't mean talking
pretty things; I mean a serious talk."

Immediately his expression grew a little
frightened.

"Don't be afraid," she said, "it's about
myself that I want to talk to you."

"About you?" he said, once more serene.
"Then it's bound to be charming."

"Wait! Wait!" she exclaimed. "Perhaps you won't say that when you have
heard me."

"What could you tell me now that would
surprise me? Haven't we told each other
273

everything, after being together for so many days?"

"So far as I'm concerned, I've scarcely said anything but *Amen*," said Annette, laughing. "You do all the talking."

"Oh! the bad girl!" exclaimed Roger. "Isn't it you that I talk about?"

"Yes, it's about me, *too*. And you even speak for me."

"You think that I talk too much?" asked Roger innocently.

Annette bit her lips. .

"No, no, my dear Roger, I love it when you talk. But when you talk about me, I just listen to you; and it is so beautiful, so beautiful that I say, 'So be it!' But it's not true."

"You are the first woman to complain of her picture being beautiful."

"I should prefer it to be me. It's not a beautiful picture that you are going to hang up in your family home, Roger. I am a living woman, who has her desires, her passions, and her thoughts. Are you sure that she can come into your home with all her baggage?"

"I am taking you with my eyes closed."

"I am asking you to open them."

"I see your limpid soul, revealed in your face."

"Poor Roger! Good Roger! . . . You don't want to look."

"I love you. That's enough for me."

"I love you too. And that isn't enough for me."

"It's not enough?" he asked in a tone of consternation.

"No. I have to see."

"What is it you want to see?"

"I want to see *how* you love me."

"I love you more than everything else in the world."

"Naturally! You couldn't do less. But I am not asking you *how much*, I am asking you *how* you love me. . . . Yes, I know that you want me; but what is it, precisely, that you want to make of your Annette?"

"Make her half of myself."

"There you are! . . . Now the point is, my friend, that I am not a half. I am a whole Annette."

"That's just a way of speaking. I mean that you are me, and that I am you."

"No, no, don't be me, Roger! Let me be that!"

"When we unite our lives, won't we make them one?"

"That's what worries me. I am afraid I can't quite do that."

"What's troubling you, Annette? What are these ideas? You love me, don't you? You love me? That's the essential thing! Don't bother about the rest. The rest is my business. You'll see, I shall arrange— I, and my family that will be yours—we shall arrange your life so well that you will have nothing to do but let yourself be carried along."

Annette was looking at the ground and tracing letters in the dirt with her toe. She was smiling.

(He didn't understand at all, the dear boy. . . .)

She raised her eyes to Roger, who, with perfect tranquillity, was awaiting her response. She said:

"Roger, look at me. Haven't I good legs?"

"Good and beautiful," said he.

"That!" she said, menacing him with her finger, "that is not the question. . . . Am I not a strong walker?"

"Of course," he said. "And I like you to be."

"Well, then, do you think that I am going to let myself be carried? . . . You are very kind, very kind, and I thank you; but let me walk! I am not one of those who fear the fatigues of the road. To take them away from me is to take away my appetite for life. I rather have the impression that you and your family would like to free me from the trouble of acting and of choosing, would like to arrange everything in advance in prescribed pigeon-holes, very comfortably—your life, their life, my life—the whole future. I shouldn't want that. I don't want it. I feel that I am at the beginning. I am seeking. I know that I have need of seeking, of seeking myself."

Roger's air was benevolent and bantering.

"And what can you seek?"

He saw here the crotchets of a young girl. She felt it, and said in a provoked tone:

"Don't make fun of me! . . . I don't amount to much, I don't pretend that I do. But after all I know what I am, and that I have a life . . . a poor little life. . . . It's not so long, a lifetime, and one has it only once. . . . I have the right. . . . No, not the right if you will! that seems egotistical. . . . It is my duty not to lose it, not to throw it away at random. . . ."

Instead of being touched, he assumed a hurt air.

"You think that you are throwing it away at random? Is your life going to be lost? Won't it have a fine, a very beautiful purpose?"

"Beautiful, no doubt. . . . But what? What do you offer me?"

Once again he ardently described his political career, the future of which he dreamed, his great personal and social ambitions. She listened to him talk, then, gently stopping him in the middle (for of such a subject he was never weary), she said:

"Yes, Roger. Certainly. That is very, very interesting. But to tell you the truth—no, don't be ruffled—I haven't quite as much faith as you in this political cause to which you are consecrating yourself."

"What! you don't believe in it? But you did believe in it when I spoke to you about it those first times that I saw you in Paris. . . ."

"I have changed a little," said she.

"What has changed you? . . . No, no, it's not possible. . . . You will change back again. My generous Annette couldn't be disinterested in the cause of the people, in the reform of society!"

"But I am not disinterested in it," she replied. "What I am disinterested in is the political cause."

"They are the same thing."

"Not entirely."

"The victory of one will be the victory of the other."

"I rather doubt it."

"Yet it is the only way of serving progress and the people."

(Annette thought: "While serving himself." But she reproached herself for it.)

"I see other ways."

"What are they?"

"The oldest is still the best. Like those
who followed Christ, to give all, to leave
all behind, in order to go to the people."

"What a utopia!"

"Yes, I believe you. You are not a
Utopian, Roger. I thought that you were
at first; I think so no longer. In politics
you have the sense of reality. With your
great talent, I am perfectly sure of your
future success. If I doubt the cause, I
don't doubt you. You will have a splendid
career. I can see you already at the head
of a party, an applauded orator, winning a
majority in Parliament, a minister . . ."

"Stop!" he said. ". . . *Macbeth, you
will be King!* . . ."

"Yes, I am something of a witch . . .
for others. But what vexes me is that I
am not for myself."

"Yet it's not so difficult. If I become minister, that concerns you too. . . . Now see here, frankly, wouldn't that please you?"

"What? To be a minister? Heavens above! Not in the least! . . . Forgive me, Roger . . . it would make me glad for your sake, of course. And if I were with you, you may be sure that I would play my part to the best of my ability, and I would be happy to help you. . . . But (you wanted me to be frank, didn't you?) I must confess that such a life would not fill my life, not at all."

"Of course, I understand that. The woman best fitted in the world to share a life of political activity—take my admirable mother for example!—couldn't limit herself to that. Her real task is in the home. And her proper vocation is motherhood."

"I know," said Annette. "We shan't argue about that vocation. But . . . (I am afraid of what I am going to say, I am afraid that you won't understand me) . . . I don't know yet what motherhood will bring me. I am very fond of children. I think that I would be very much attached to my own. . . . (You don't like that word? Yes, I seem cold to you. . . .) Perhaps I would be completely wrapped up in them. . . . It is possible. . . . I don't know. . . . But I shouldn't like to say something that I don't feel. And to be perfectly frank, this 'vocation' is not yet entirely awakened in me. While still waiting for life to reveal something of which I am ignorant, it doesn't seem to me that a woman ought, in any case, to bury her whole life in this love of children. . . . (Don't raise your eyebrows! . . .) I am convinced that it is possible to love one's child, loyally perform one's domestic task, and still keep enough of oneself — as one ought to — for the most essential thing."

"The most essential?"

"One's soul."

"I don't understand."

"How can one make one's inner life understood? Words are so uncertain, so obscure, botched! The soul . . . It is ridiculous to speak of the soul! What does it mean? I can't explain what it is. But it is. It is what I am, Roger, the truest and deepest."

"Don't you give me what is truest and deepest?"

"I can't give all," she said.

"Then you don't love me."

"Yes, Roger, I love you. But no one can give all."

"You are not enough in love. When one is in love, one doesn't think of holding back any part of oneself. Love . . . love . . . love . . ."

And he soared off into one of his great speeches. Annette heard him celebrate, in moving terms, the whole gift of self, the joy of sacrificing for the happiness of the beloved. And she thought:

(My dear, why do you say all that? Do you think I don't know it? Do you think that I couldn't sacrifice myself for you, if it were necessary, and find my joy in it? But on one condition: that you don't demand it. . . . Why do you demand it? . . . Why do you seem to expect it as your right? Why haven't you confidence in me, in my love?)

After he had finished, she said:

"That is very beautiful. . . . I wouldn't be capable, you know, of expressing these things as well as you. But perhaps, on occasion, I wouldn't be incapable of feeling them. . . ."

He exclaimed: "Perhaps! On occasion!"

"You find that very little, don't you? It is more than you think. . . . But I don't like to promise more . . . (perhaps it is less) . . . than I can fulfill. I don't know in advance. We must trust each other. We are upright people. We love each other, Roger. We shall do all that we can."

Again he raised his arms.

"All that we can! . . ."

She smiled and continued.

"Do you want to trust me? I need to draw on my credit. I have much to ask. . . ."

He was prudent: "Go ahead!"

"I love you, Roger, but I should like to be sincere. From my childhood I have lived alone a good deal and enjoyed a great deal of freedom. My father left in me a spirit of independence, which I haven't abused, because it seemed quite natural to me, and because it was wholesome. So I have acquired certain habits of mind that I should find difficult, now, to do without. I know that I am rather different from the majority of young girls of my class. Yet I believe that what I feel they feel too; only I dare to say it, and I have a clearer conscience. You ask me to unite my life with yours. It is my wish. For each of us it is our most profound desire to find our beloved mate. And it seems to me that you could be that mate, Roger . . . if . . . if you wished . . ."

"If I wished!" he exclaimed. "That's a good joke! I don't do anything but wish! . . ."

"If you *truly* wished to be my mate. It is not a joke. Reflect! . . . To unite our lives means to suppress either one or the other. . . . What do you offer me? . . . You aren't aware of it, because the world has long been used to these inequalities.

But they are new to me. . . . You do not
come to me with only your affection. You
come to me with your family, your friends,
your clients, and your relatives, with your
course mapped out, your career fixed, with
your party and its dogmas, your family and
its traditions,—with a whole world that is
yours, a whole world that is you. And I,
who have a world too, who am also a
world,—you say to me: 'Abandon your
world! Throw it away, and enter into
mine!' I am ready to come, Roger, but I
must come whole. Do you accept me as I
am?"

"I want all," said he. "It was you, just
now, who said that you could not give me
all."

"You don't understand. I say: 'Do you
accept me free? And do you accept all
of me?'"

"Free?" responded Roger circumspectly.
"Everybody has been free in France since
'89. . . ." (Annette smiled: "The old
platitude! . . .") "But, after all, we must
understand each other. It is certainly evident that from the moment you marry you

will not be completely free. By that act you will have contracted obligations."

"I don't like that word very much," said Annette, "but I am not afraid of the thing. I should joyously and freely take my part in the trials and labors of the man I loved, in the duties of our common life. But I won't renounce, on that account, the duties of my own life."

"And what other duties are there? After what you have told me and what I think I know, your life, my dear Annette, your life that until now has been so placid and so calm, does not seem to me to have experienced any very great exigencies? What could it demand? Is it your work that you mean? Would you like to go on with it? I confess that that kind of activity seems wrong to me, for a woman. At least, as a vocation. It's bothersome, in the home. . . . But I can't believe that you are afflicted with this gift from Heaven. You are too human, and too well balanced."

"No, it isn't a question of a special vocation. That would be simple, for then one would have to follow it. . . . The demand, the exigence (as you say) of my life is less easy to formulate: for it is less precise and much more vast. It is a question of the right laid upon every living soul: the right to change."

Roger cried: "To change!   To change love?"

"Even while always remaining faithful, as I have said, to a single love, the soul has the right to change. . . . Yes, I know, Roger, that the word 'change' frightens you. . . . It disturbs me, too. . . . When the passing hour is beautiful, I should like never to stir. One sighs that it cannot be held forever! . . . And yet, Roger, one ought not to do it; and, first of all, one cannot. One does not remain stationary. One lives, one goes forward, one is pushed, —one must, must advance! This does no injury to love; one takes that along. But love should not wish to hold us back, shut up with it in the immobile sweetness of a single thought. A beautiful love may last for a whole lifetime, but it cannot entirely fill it. Think, my dear Roger, that while

still loving you I might find myself some
day, perhaps (I find myself already),
cramped within your circle of action and
thought. I would never dream of arguing
with you the excellence of your choice.
But would it be just for it to be imposed
on me? And don't you find it equitable
to grant me the right of opening the window, if I haven't enough air,—and even
the door, a little—(oh! I won't go far)—
and for me to have my own little province
of activity, my intellectual interests, my
friendships, not to remain confined to one
point of the globe, to the same horizon, but
to try and enlarge it, to seek a change of
air, to emigrate. . . . (I say: if it is
necessary. . . . I don't know yet. But in
any case I need to feel that I am free to
do it, that I am free to wish, free to
breathe, free . . . free to be free . . . even
if I never make use of my liberty.) . . .
Forgive me, Roger, perhaps you find this
need absurd and childish. It is not, I assure you; it is the most profound need of
my being, the breath that gives me life.
If it were taken away from me, I should

die. . . . I can do everything, for love.
. . . But constraint kills me. And the idea
of constraint makes me a rebel. No, the
union of two beings ought not to become
a mutual enchainment. It should be a
twofold blooming. I should like each, instead of being jealous of the other's free
development, to be happy in assisting it.
Would you be, Roger? Would you know
how to love me enough to love me free,
free of you? . . ."

(She was thinking: "I should be yours
only the more! . . .")

Roger was listening to her anxiously,
nervous, and a little vexed. Any man
would have been. Annette should have
been capable of more adroitness. In her
need of frankness and her fear of decep-
tion, she was always led into exaggerating
the most startling features of her thought.
But a stronger love than Roger's would
not have set this all at naught. Roger, his
self-love touched above all, wavered between two sentiments: that of not taking
this feminine caprice seriously, and the
annoyance that he felt at this moral insur-

rection.   He had not perceived its passionate appeal to his heart.   All that he
understood of it was that it was a sort of
obscure menace and attack upon his proprietary rights.   If he had possessed more
cunning in his management of women, he
would have hidden his secret vexation,
and promised, promised, promised . . . all
that Annette desired.   "Lover's promises,
as many as the wind will carry.   Why
then be niggardly? . . ." But Roger, who
had his faults, also had his virtues: he was,
as they say, "a simple young fellow," too
much filled with himself to be well acquainted with women, with whom he had
had recent dealings.   He lacked the skill
to hide his vexation.   And when Annette
awaited his generous answer, she suffered
the disappointment of seeing that while listening to her he had thought only of himself.

"Annette," said he, "I confess that I
can scarcely understand what you ask of
me.   You talk of our marriage as of a
prison, and your one idea seems to be to
escape from it.   My house has no bars at

the windows, and it is large enough for one
to be comfortable in it. But one cannot
live with all the doors wide open, and my
house is made to be lived in. You talk to
me about leaving it, about having your
individual life, your personal relationships,
your friends, and even, if I have rightly
understood, of your privilege to leave the
home at will, in search of Heaven knows
what you fail to find there, until it happens to please you to come back again some
day. . . . This can't be serious, Annette!
You haven't thought about it! No man
could grant his wife a position that would
be so humiliating for him and so equivocal
for her."

These reflections were not, perhaps, lacking in good sense. But there are times
when perfectly dry good sense, with no
intuition of the heart, is a kind of nonsense. Annette, somewhat ruffled, answered
with a proud frigidity that masked her
emotion:

"Roger, it is necessary to have faith in
the woman one loves; when one marries
her, one must not do her the wrong of

believing that she would not have the same
care as yourself for your honor. Do you
think that such a woman as myself would
lend herself to an equivocation in order to
humiliate you? Any humiliation for you
would be a humiliation for her as well.
And the freer she were, the more bound
she would feel to watch over that part of
yourself which you had confided to her.
You will have to esteem me more highly.
Aren't you capable of having confidence
in me?"

He felt the danger of alienating her by
his doubts; and, telling himself that after
all there was no need of attaching an exaggerated importance to these feminine ideas,
and that there would be time later to correct them—(if she remembered them!)—
he returned to his first idea, which was to
take the whole thing as a joke. So he believed that he was doing very well, when
he said gallantly:

"Perfect confidence, Annette! I believe
in your fair eyes. Only swear to me that
you will love me always, that you will love

me alone! I ask nothing more of you!"

But the little Cordelia, who could not reconcile herself to this trifling fashion of avoiding the honest response on which her life depended, stiffened against this impossible pledge.

"No, Roger, I can't, I can't swear that. I love you very much. But I cannot promise something that does not depend upon myself. It would mean deceiving you; and I shall never deceive you. I promise you simply to hide nothing from you. And if the time comes when I love you no longer, or love another, you will be the first to know it,—even before that other. And you do the same! Oh, Roger! let us be honest!"

That was scarcely possible. Embarrassing truth was something to which the house of Brissot was not accustomed. When it knocked on the door, they hastened to send word:

"Everyone is out!"

Roger did not fail to do it. He cried:

"My dear, how pretty you are! . . . There, let us talk of something else! . . ."

XIII

'Annette returned to the house, disappointed. She had cherished great hopes of a frank talk. Although she had anticipated resistance, she had counted on Roger's heart illumining his mind. The most distressing thing was not that Roger had not understood, but that he had not made the least effort to understand. He seemed to see nothing pathetic in the question for Annette. He was all on the surface, and he saw everything in his own image. Nothing could be more painful to a woman with a strong inner life.

She did not deceive herself. Roger had been embarrassed, irritated by Annette's words, but he had completely failed to perceive their seriousness; he considered them inconsequential. He thought that Annette had bizarre and rather paradoxical ideas, that she was "original": it was troublesome. Madame and Mademoiselle Brissot knew how to be superior without

being "original." But one could not demand this perfection in everyone. Annette
had other qualities,—that, perhaps, Roger
did not place so high, but to which he
clung (it must be said) much more firmly
at the moment. In this preference the
body had a greater share than the mind;
but the mind, too, had its share. Roger
took a keen delight in Annette's heedless
ardor, when it was not exercised on subjects embarrassing to him. He was not
disturbed. Annette, in her uprightness, had
shown him that she loved him. He was
convinced that she would not be able to
disengage herself from him.

He little suspected the drama of conscience that was being played out at his
side. In truth, Annette loved him so much
that she could not bring herself to think
him such a sorry figure. She wished to
believe herself mistaken. She tested other
possibilities, she tried to do her best. If
Roger would not grant her an independent
life, at least what part would he give her
in his own? But the new conclusions at
which she found herself compelled to ar-

rive were discouraging. Roger's naïve egotism relegated her, in fine, to the dining
table, the drawing-room, and the bed. He
was very ready to tell her, prettily, about
his affairs; but all she had to do, thereafter, was to approve of them. He was
no more disposed to concede to his wife the
rights of a collaborator who might discuss
his political activities with him and modify
them, than he was to permit her a social
activity different from his own. It seemed
to him perfectly natural—(it was always
done)—that the woman who loved him
should give him her whole life, and that
she should receive only a portion of his.
At the bottom of his nature he held that
old masculine belief in his own superiority
which made him feel that what he gave
was of a finer essence. But he would not
have admitted it, for he was a good fellow
and a gallant Frenchman. If it happened
that Annette presumed to base certain
feminine rights on the example of the
husband, Roger would smilingly say:

"It is not the same thing."

"Why?" Annette would ask.

And Roger would avoid a response. A conviction that one does not discuss suffers less danger of being shaken. Roger's conviction was firmly rooted. And Annette chose the wrong course to make him doubt himself. Her advances, her efforts to find a mutual ground of understanding, after her useless attempt to impose her ideas on him, were interpreted by Roger as a fresh proof of the power that he had over her. And he even grew vain. Suddenly Annette would become irritated, and a quivering note would mark her speech. Roger would pull himself up short, and return to the method that, in his opinion, had been so successful: he would laughingly promise all that was demanded of him. It is the tone, they say, that puts the song across. That was the case with Roger. Annette was conscious of the contempt.

Other more serious questions arose. Annette's intimacy with Sylvie had been dangerously menaced. It was evident that the free-minded girl would not be readily welcomed into this circle, and that the little seamstress would be still less so. Never would the vain, stiff-necked Brissots admit, for themselves or for their daughter-in-law, any such scandalous evidence of relationship. It would have to be hidden. And Sylvie would be no more ready to do this than Annette. Each had her pride, and each was proud of the other. Annette loved Roger, and she wanted him with a more burning desire than she confessed to herself; but she would never sacrifice her Sylvie to him. She had loved her too much; and if this love, perhaps, had waned, she did not forget that at moments it had made her touch the ultimate depths of passion:—(she knew it, she alone; even Sylvie suspected only half the truth). But, in the hours of her mutual confidence with Roger, Annette had told him much too much. Then Roger had seemed amused, touched. . . . Yes, but on the condition that all this belonged to the past. He had no intention of seeing a prolongation of this compromising sisterhood. Secretly, he had even decided to put an end to it, gently, without appearing to take a hand in the affair. He did not wish to share his wife's intimacy with anyone. *His* wife . . . *"This dog is mine. . . ."* Like all his family, he had a very keen sense of what belonged to him.

As Annette's visit grew longer, this possessive grasp grew tighter,—from certain affectionate externalities with which they surrounded her. What the Brissots possessed, they possessed. The domestic despotism of the two women sharply manifested itself daily in a thousand minute details. Their "mind," as the saying goes, was "made up" on everything, whether it was a question of the household or the world, of everyday existence or of great problems of the moral life. It was screwed down, fixed, once for all. Everything was prescribed: what must be praised, what must be rejected,—especially what must be rejected! Such ostracisms! What men, what things, what ways of thinking or of acting, were judged, condemned without appeal, and for eternity! The tone and the smile removed the desire to argue. They had an air of saying (they often said, in so many words):

"There are not two ways of thinking, my dear child."

Or, when Annette none the less tried to show that there was a way also of her own:

"My dear, how amusing you are!"

Which had the effect of making her instantly shut her mouth.

They already treated her as a daughter of the house, not quite thoroughly trained, whom they were instructing. They instructed her regarding the order and course of the Brissot days, months, and seasons, regarding their relatives in the province and their relatives in Paris, their duties of kinship, their calls, their dinners, and the endless chain of those social tasks, about which the women complained, and of which they were very proud, because the harassment of this perpetual activity gave them the illusion that they were being of some service. This mechanical life, these false relationships, this perpetual convention, were all intolerable to Annette. Everything seemed regulated in advance: work and pleasure,— for they had their pleasures too,—but regulated in advance! . . . Hurrah for unfore-

seen ills that released one from the program!   But there was little hope of re-
lease, even on the score of ills.   Annette
felt herself bricked in, like a stone in a
wall!   Sand and lime.   Roman cement.
Brissot mortar. . . .

She exaggerated the rigorousness of this
life.   Chance and the unexpected played
their parts in it, as in all lives.   The Mesdames Brissot were more redoubtable in
words than in fact; they pretended to direct everything; but it was not impossible,
if one attacked their weak spots, anointed
them, flattered and worshipped them, to
lead them by the nose; a cunning girl
might have said to herself, while evaluating them at their proper worth:

"Keep on talking!   I'll do things my
own way!"

One would have thought that a tena-
cious energy, like Annette's, could never be
stifled.   But Annette was passing through
that nervous fever of women who, by dint
of staring too fixedly at the object which
preoccupies them, cease to see it as it is.
From a few words heard during the day-

time, she forged monsters when she was
alone at night. She was appalled at the
battle which she had to wage continually,
and she repeated to herself that she would
never succeed in defending herself against
them all. She did not feel strong enough.
She mistrusted her own energy. She was
afraid of her own nature, of those unexpected oscillations by which her troubled
mind continued to be shaken, of those sharp
gusts that she could not explain. And, indeed, they sprang from the complexity of
her rich being whose new harmony could
be slowly realized only by living; but, in
the meantime, there was danger of their
plunging her into many surprises of violence and weakness, of the flesh and of the
mind, of the insidious hazards of fate, ambushed beneath the stones of the road. . . .

The basis of her trouble was that she
was no longer sure of her love. She no
longer knew. . . . She no longer loved,
and yet she still loved. Her mind and
heart—her mind and senses—were at battle. The mind saw too clearly; it was dis-
illusioned. But the heart was not; and the

body was irritated when it saw that it was
going to lose what it coveted; passion
grumbled:

"I do not want to renounce! . . ."

Annette felt this revolt, and she was
humiliated by it; her natural violence re-
acted forcibly, appealing to her wounded
pride. She said:

"I love him no longer! . . ."

And her now hostile glance espied in
Roger the reasons for no longer loving him.

Roger saw nothing. He surrounded Annette with kindnesses, with flowers, with
gallant attentions. But he thought that the
game was won. Not for an instant did he
dream of the proud savage soul that was
observing him, from behind its veil, burning to give itself—but to him who would
utter the mysterious password which shows
that one is recognized. He did not utter
it; and for a reason. On the contrary, he
uttered irreflective words that, without her
showing it, wounded Annette to the heart.
The instant after, he no longer remembered
what he had said. But Annette, who had
not seemed to hear, could have repeated

them to him ten days, ten years later. She kept the memory of them fresh, and the wound open. It was in spite of herself, for she was generous, and she reproached herself for not knowing how to forget. But the best of women may pardon intimate offenses; she never forgets them.

Day by day, rents appeared in the fine cloth woven by love. The cloth remained stretched tight, but the least breath made disquieting shivers pass over it. Annette, observing Roger in the family circle, with his family traits, the hardness, the dryness of certain of his speeches and his contempt for humble people, said to herself:

"He is fading. At the end of a few years there will remain nothing of what I love in him."

And since she loved him still, she wished to avoid the bitter disillusion, the degrading conflicts between them that she foresaw, if they were united.

Two nights before Easter, her decision was made. A miserable night. There were many desires to be vanquished, obsti-

nate hope that did not wish to die had to
be trodden under foot. She had, in imagination, built her nest with Roger. So many
dreams of happiness that they had whispered to each other! Renounce them!
Recognize that they had been mistaken!
Admit that one was not made for happiness! . . .

For that is what she told herself in her
discouragement. Another, in her place,
would not have been cast down. Why was
she not capable of accepting it? Why
could she not sacrifice a part of her nature?
. . . But no, she could not! How badly
life is arranged! One cannot live without
mutual affection; no more can one live
without independence. The one is as
sacred as the other. One as much as the
other is necessary to the air we breathe.
How can they be reconciled? They say to
you: "Sacrifice! If you do not sacrifice,
you do not love enough. . . ." But it is
almost always those who are capable of a
great love who are also the most enamoured
of independence. For in them, all is
strong. And if they sacrifice to their love

the principle of their pride, they feel themselves degraded even in their love, they dishonor love. . . . No, it is not so simple as the morality of humility would have us believe—or that of pride,—the Christian or the Nietzschean doctrine. In us a strength is not opposed to a weakness, a virtue to a vice; it is two forces confronting two virtues, two duties. . . . The sole true morality, according to the true life, would be a morality of harmony. But, so far, human society has known only a morality of repression and renunciation, —tempered by lies. Annette could not lie. . . .

What was to be done? . . . To escape from equivocation as quickly as possible, at any price! Since she was convinced that it would be impossible to live in this union, to break it the next day! . . .

Break! . . . She imagined to herself the family's stupefaction, the scandal. . . . That was nothing. . . . But Roger's grief. . . . Immediately she pictured to herself in the darkness the image of his beloved face. . . . At this vision a new surge of

passion swept everything away. . . . . Annette, burning and icy, motionless in her
bed, upon her back, with her eyes open,
suppressed the beatings of her heart. . . .

"Roger," she implored, "my Roger, forgive me! . . . Oh! If I could spare you
this pain! . . . I cannot, I cannot! . . ."

Then she was bathed in such a flood of
love and of remorse that she nearly went
running to fling herself at the foot of
Roger's bed, to kiss his hands, and say to
him:

"I will do everything you wish. . . ."

What! She still loved him? . . . She
rebelled. . . .

"No, no! I don't love him any
more! . . ."

She lied to herself furiously. . . .

"I don't love him any more! . . ."

In vain! . . . She still loved him. She
loved him more than ever. Perhaps not
with the noblest part of her—(but what is
noble, and what is not?)—Yes! with the
noblest too, and with the least! Body and
soul! . . . If one could only stop loving

when one stopped respecting! How comfortable that would be! . . . But to suffer
at the hands of the beloved has never ex-
empted one from loving him: one feels it
only the more cruelly when one is forced
to love him! . . . Annette was suffering
in her wounded love—from lack of confidence, lack of faith in herself, lack of
Roger's profound love. She was suffering
from the bitter consciousness of all the
destroyed hopes which she had hatched and
which would never see the light of day.
It was because she loved Roger so ardently
that she insisted on making him accept her
independence. She wanted to be to him
more than a woman who abdicates, passive
in the union,—a free and sure companion.
He took no stock in it. She felt within
herself a sorrow, an anger of offended
passion. . . .

"No! no! I love him no longer! I
ought not to, I don't want to. . . ."

But her strength crumpled, and, even
before she could finish her cry of rebellion,
she wept. . . . In the night, in silence.

. . . Beneath the ice of reason, alas! she was on fire. . . . There was that which she did not wish to say: what joy she would have found in sacrificing to him all that she had, even her independence, if only he had made a generous move, a gesture, a simple gesture, to sacrifice himself, rather than to sacrifice her! . . . She would not have let him do it. She would have demanded no more than an outburst of the heart, a proof of true love. But that proof, although he loved her in his own way, he was incapable of giving. It did not enter his thoughts. He had judged Annette's desire as a feminine requirement that must be received smilingly, but in which there was not much sense. What could she wish? Why the devil was she crying? Because she loved him? Well then? . . .

"You love me, don't you? You love me? That is the essential thing. . . ."

Ah! that word, she had not forgotten that either! . . .

Annette smiled amid her tears. Poor Roger! He was what he was. One could not grudge him that. But one does not change. Neither he, nor I. We cannot live together. . . .

She dried her eyes.

"Come now, one must put a stop to this. . . ."

XIV

After a white night—(she had drowsed
for only an hour or two at dawn)—Annette arose, resolute. With the light of
day, calm returned to her. She dressed
herself and did her hair methodically,
coldly, shutting out of her mind everything
that might awaken its doubts, attentive to
her toilet, which she made with an even
more than ordinary meticulous attention to
correct detail.

About nine o'clock Roger knocked gaily
at her door. Following his morning cus-
tom, he had come to take her for a walk.

They set out, escorted by a gamboling
dog. They took a road that led beneath
the trees. The young, verdant woods were
shot through with sunlight. The branches
were alive with the songs and cries of birds.
Every step sent them flying; there were
beatings of wings, rustlings of leaves, clash-
ing of branches, frenzied flights through
the forest. The excited dog snapped and

sniffed and zig-zagged. Jays were bicker-
ing. In the cupola of an oak, two ring-
doves were cooing. And far away, the
cuckoo was circling, circling, farther, then
nearer, tirelessly repeating his ancient jest.
It was the outburst of spring fever. . . .

Roger, noisy, very gay, laughing, and
exciting his dog, was himself like a big,
happy dog. Annette followed silently, at
a few paces. She was thinking:

"Here! . . . No, yonder at the turning. . . ."

She was watching Roger. She was listening to the forest. How different all would
be, after she had spoken! . . . The turn
was passed. She had not spoken. . . . She
said: "Roger . . ." in an uncertain, trembling voice, almost a whisper. . . . He
did not hear it, he noticed nothing. Stoop-
ing down in front of her, he gathered some
violets, and he talked, talked. . . . She
repeated: "Roger!" this time in such an
accent of distress that he turned around,
startled. At once he saw the pallor of her
gravely serious face; he came to her. . . .
He was afraid already. She said:

"Roger, we must separate."

His features expressed stupefaction and dismay. He stammered:

"What's that you say?   What's that you say?"

Avoiding his glance, she repeated firmly:

"We must separate, Roger; it is sad, but we must.   I have come to see that it is impossible, impossible for me to be your wife. . . ."

She wanted to go on, but he prevented her.

"No, no, that's not true! . . . Be still! Be still!   You are mad! . . ."

"I must go away, Roger," she said.

He shouted: "Go away, you! . . . I don't want you to! . . ."

He had seized her arms, and was squeezing them brutally.   Then he caught sight of her proud face, obstinate and glacial; he felt that he was lost, he let go, he begged pardon, he prayed, he pleaded.

"Annette!   My little Annette!   Stay, stay! . . . No, it isn't possible. . . . But what has happened?   What have I done?"

Pity reappeared on the firm face. She said:

"Let's sit down, Roger. . . ."

(He seated himself docilely beside her on a mossy bank: his eyes never left her, imploring at every word).

". . . Be calm, everything must be explained. . . . Be calm, I beg of you! . . . Believe me that I have to use all my strength to be. . . . I could not speak unless I forced myself to do so. . . ."

"But don't speak," he cried. "It is madness! . . ."

"It is necessary."

He tried to close her mouth. She pulled herself away. Despite the disturbance within her, her resolution seemed so inflexible that she imposed it on Roger who, abandoning the struggle, beaten and haggard, listened to her words, without daring to look at her. Annette, in a voice that seemed impassive, cold and mournful, but which was marked by sharp breaks, and which once or twice stopped to take breath along the way,—said what she had decided to say, in words that were clear, studied, and moderate, but which seemed all the more implacable for that. . . . She had sincerely wanted to test out whether they could live together. She hoped so at first, she wished it with all her heart. She had seen that this dream could not be realized. Too many things separated them. Too many differences in their surroundings and in their thoughts. She laid the blame at her own door; she had definitely recognized that she could not live a married life. She had conceptions of life, of independence, which did not accord with Roger's. Perhaps Roger was right. The majority of men, perhaps of women even, thought as he did. She was wrong, no doubt. But right or wrong, that was how she was. It was useless for her to cause another's misery and her own. She was made to live alone. She freed Roger from all promises made to her, and took back her own freedom. For the rest, they were not bound. Everything had been upright between them. They must separate uprightly, as friends. . . .

While speaking, she stared at the grass at her feet; she was very careful not to

look at Roger. But, as she spoke, she heard
his gasping breath, and it was a sore trial
for her to go on to the end. When she
had finished, she risked looking at him. In
her turn, she was smitten. Roger's face
was like that of a drowning man: flushed,
breathing noisily, he had not the strength
to cry out. Awkwardly he moved his
clenched hands, sought and found his
breath, and groaned:

"No, no, no, no, I cannot, I cannot . . ."

And he burst into sobs.

From a field by the edge of the woods,
they heard the voice of a peasant, the noise
of a plow-share. Annette, overcome with
emotion, seized Roger by the arm and drew
him away from the road, into the bushes,
then further into the midst of the forest.
Roger, devoid of strength, let himself be
led, repeating:

"I cannot, I cannot. . . . What is going
to become of me? . . ."

Tenderly she tried to keep him from
speaking. But he was overwhelmed by his
despair: the misery of his love, of his pride,

the public humiliation, the ruined happiness that was to be his lot,—all these were
at once commingled. This big child who
had been spoiled by life, who had never
seen anything resist his desire, broke down
at this defeat: it was a catastrophe, a crumbling of all his certainties; he was losing
faith in himself, he was losing his foothold, there was no way for him to turn.
Annette, touched by this great grief, was
saying:

"My sweetheart . . . my sweetheart.
. . . Don't cry! . . . You have, you will
have a beautiful life . . . you will have
no need of me."

He continued to moan.

"I can't do without you. I no longer
believe in anything. . . . I no longer believe in my life. . . ."

And he flung himself on his knees.

"Stay! Stay with me! . . . I will do
what you want . . . everything that you
want. . . ."

Annette knew perfectly well that he was
making promises that he could not fulfill,
but she was touched. Gently she replied:

"No, my friend, you are saying it sincerely, but you couldn't do it, or you would suffer because of it, and I should suffer too; life would be a perpetual conflict. . . ."

When he saw that he could not shake her resolution, he burst into tears at her feet, like a child. Annette was pierced by pity and by love. Her energy melted. She tried to remain firm, but she could not resist these tears. She thought of herself no longer; she thought only of him. She caressed that dear head resting against her legs, and she said tender words to him. She lifted up her big, unhappy boy, she dried his eyes with her handkerchief, she took him by the arm again, she compelled him to walk. He was so prostrated that he surrendered himself, knowing only how to weep. As they went along, the branches of the trees lashed their faces. They went into the woods, without seeing, without knowing where. Annette felt emotion and love rising within her. Supporting Roger, she said:

"Don't cry! . . . my dear! . . . my little one. It tears me to pieces. . . . I

can't bear it. . . . Don't cry! . . . I love
you. . . . I love you, my poor little
Roger. . . ."

And he answered

"No. . . .!"

in the midst of his tears.

"Yes! I love you, I love you, a thousand
times more than you have ever loved me.
. . . What do you want me to do? . . .
Oh! I shall do it. . . . Roger, my
Roger. . . ."

And now as they were walking, they
came out of the woods, and found themselves at the fence of the Rivière property,
near the old house. Annette recognized it.
. . . She looked at Roger. . . . And suddenly passion invaded her whole body. A
wind of fire. A drunkenness of the senses,
like the intoxication of an acacia in bloom.
. . . She ran towards the door, holding
Roger by the hand. They entered the deserted habitation. The blinds were shut.
Coming in out of the broad daylight, they
were blinded. Roger bumped against the
furniture. Without seeing and without
thinking, he let himself be guided by the

burning hand that led him through the
darkness of the ground floor rooms. Annette did not hesitate, her destiny drew her
on. . . . Into the room at the back, the
room of the two sisters, in which from the
past autumn there still floated the perfume
of their two bodies, toward the big bed,
where they had both slept, she went with
him; and, in a passion of pity and of joy,
—she gave herself to him.

XV

When they awakened from their over-whelming intoxication, their eyes were accustomed to darkness. The room seemed lighted. Rays of sunlight came dancing through the slits in the blinds, reminding them of the fine day outside. Roger was covering Annette's unclothed body with kisses; he was giving voice to his gratitude in inarticulate words. . . .

But after he had spoken, he suddenly fell silent, his face resting against Annette's side. . . . Annette, silent and motionless, was dreaming. . . . Outside, in the rose-bush by the wall, bees were buzzing. . . . And, like a song receding in the distance, Annette heard Roger's love take wings. . . .

Already he loved her less. Roger, too, felt it with shame and annoyance; but he was unwilling to admit it. Fundamentally, he was shocked that Annette had given herself. . . . Ridiculous exigence of man! He desires the woman, and when she sincerely surrenders herself to him, he almost regards her over-generous act as an infidelity! . . .

Annette leaned towards him, lifted up his head, looked into his eyes for a long time, said nothing, and smiled a melancholy smile. When he felt this glance piercing him to his very soul, he sought to deceive her. He intended to appear thoroughly enamoured. He said:

"Now, Annette, you cannot go: I *must* marry you."

Annette's sad smile reappeared. She had read him perfectly. . . .

"No, my friend," said she, "you *must* nothing."

He recovered himself.

"I want . . ."

But she replied: "I am going to go."

"Why?" he asked.

And before she spoke he already understood her reasons for departure. However, he felt obliged to dispute them afresh. She put her hand over his mouth; and he kissed that hand with passionate anger. . . . Oh! how much he loved her! He was humiliated by his own thoughts. Had not she seen them? . . . And the sweet, moist hand that caressed his lips seemed to say:

"I have seen nothing. . . ."

From a distant village came the tolling of bells, borne upon the fitful wind. . . . After a long silence, Annette sighed. . . . Come, this time it is the end. . . . In a hushed voice she said:

"Roger, we must go back. . . ."

Their bodies drew apart. Kneeling beside the bed, he pressed his brow against Annette's bare feet. He wished to prove to her:

"I am thine."

But he did not succeed in driving away his afterthought.

He went out of the room, leaving Annette to dress. While waiting he leaned his elbows on a wall of the little entrance court, listening vaguely to the noises of the countryside and savoring the hour just passed. Importunate ideas were eclipsed. He rejoiced in the happiness of pride and sensual appeasement. He was proud of himself. He thought:

"Poor Annette!"

He corrected himself:

"Dear Annette! . . ."

She came out of the house. As calm as ever. But very pale. . . . Who can tell all that had passed during those brief moments that she had been left alone: assaults of passion, grief, renunciation? . . . Roger saw nothing of all this, he was absorbed in himself. He went to her and sought to renew his protestations. She raised a finger to her lips: Silence! . . . At the hedge that enclosed the garden she plucked a branch of hawthorn, she broke it in two, and gave him half. And as she left the Rivière estate with him, on the very threshold, she pressed her lips to Roger's.

They returned without a word, through the forest. Annette had begged him not to break the silence. He held her arm. His attitude was very tender. She was smiling, with her eyes half closed. And this time it was he who guided her steps. He did not recall that only an hour ago, at this very spot, he had wept. . . .

In the depths of the forest the dog was barking in pursuit of game. . . .

XVI

She took her departure on the following
day. Her excuse was a letter, a sudden
illness of her old aunt. The Brissots were
not completely fooled by this. For some
time they had been more suspicious than
Roger that Annette was escaping them.
But it suited their dignity not to seem to
admit this possibility, and to believe in the
reasons given for this sudden departure.
Up to the last moment they played a
comedy of brief separation and early re-
union. This constraint was painful to Annette; but Roger had begged her not to
announce her decision until later, at Paris,
and Annette admitted to herself that she
would have found it hard to inform the
Brissots by word of mouth. So, when they
took leave of each other, they exchanged
smiles, coy words and embraces from which
the heart was absent.

Roger again accompanied Annette in a
carriage to the station. They were both
sad. Roger had virtuously renewed his

request to Annette that she should marry
him; he felt that he was bound to: he was
a gentleman. Too much of a one. He
also felt that he had the right, now, to
make his authority felt,—in the interest of
Annette. He thought that because she had
given herself, because Annette had abdi-
cated, the situation between them was no
longer quite equal, and that he must now
demand marriage. Annette saw only too
clearly that, if he married her now, he
would think himself justified a thousand
times more than ever in playing her
guardian. Of course, she was grateful to
him for his correct insistence. But . . .
she refused. Roger was secretly irritated
by this. He no longer understood her.
. . . (He thought that he had always understood her!) . . . And he judged her
severely. He did not show it. But she
guessed it, with mingled sorrow and irony,
—and always tenderness. . . . (He was
still Roger! . . .)

When they had nearly arrived, she
placed her gloved hand on Roger's hand.
He started:

"Annette!"

"Let us forgive each other!" she said.

He wished to speak; he could not. Their hands remained clasped. They did not look at each other, but each knew that the other was holding back the tears, ready to flow. . . .

They were at the station; they had to be discreet. Roger installed Annette in her carriage. She was not alone in the compartment. They had to restrict themselves to commonplace courtesies; but the eyes of each were avidly seizing upon the image of the other's beloved face.

The engine whistled.

"Till we meet again!" they said.

And they were thinking: "Never!"

The train pulled out. Roger returned home in the falling night. His heart was full of sorrow and of anger. Of anger against Annette. Of anger against himself. He felt torn asunder. He felt—oh, shame!—he felt relieved. . . .

And stopping his horse on the deserted road, in contempt for himself and in contempt for love, he wept bitterly.

XVII

Annette returned home to the Boulogne house, and there she shut herself up. When the letter to the Brissots had gone off, she severed all connections with the outside world. None of her friends knew that she had returned. She opened no letters. For days she never left the floor on which she lived. Her old aunt, accustomed not to understand her and not to worry about it, respected her isolation. Her external life seemed suspended. Her other, secret life was only the more intense. Her silence was swept by storms of wounded passion. She had to be alone so that she might abandon herself to them to the point of exhaustion. She emerged from them broken, her blood drained, her mouth parched, with burning brow, and hands and feet like ice. There followed torpid periods given over to deep dreams. For days she dreamed; and she made no effort to direct her thoughts. She was invaded by a confused mass of mingled emotions. . . . A somber

melancholy, a bitter sweetness, a taste of
ashes in the mouth, disappointed hopes,
sudden flashes of memory that made her
heart leap, fits of embittered despair, pride
and passion, and a sense of ruin, of the
irremediable, of a Fate against which all
efforts are vain,—at first a crushing feeling,
then mournful, then dissolving into a
drowsiness whose distant sorrow was marked
by a strange pleasure. . . . She did not
understand. . . .

One night, in a dream, she saw herself
in a bourgeoning forest. She was alone.
She was running through the thickets.
Tree branches laid hold of her dress, damp
bushes clutched her; she freed herself, but
tore her clothes in doing so, and saw with
shame that she was half naked. She bent
to cover herself with the tatters of her
skirt. And then before her, on the ground,
she saw a small oval basket, beneath a pile
of sun-drenched leaves,—not yellow and
gold, but white as silver, like the trunk of
a birch, white with the finest linen. Deeply
moved, she looked at it, she knelt beside it.

She saw the linen begin to stir. With beating heart, she stretched out her hand. . . . Her emotion persisted. . . . She did not understand. . . .

There came a day—when she understood. . . . She was alone no longer. . . . In her a life was arising, a new life. . . .

And the weeks passed, while she brooded over her hidden universe. . . .

"Love, is it really thou? Love, thou who hast fled me when I sought to seize thee, hast thou entered into me? I hold thee, I hold thee, thou shalt not escape me; oh, my little prisoner, I hold thee in my body. Revenge thyself! Devour me! Little consuming creature, devour my vitals! Nourish thyself on my blood! Thou art myself. Thou art my dream. Since I could not find thee in this world, I have made thee with my flesh. . . . And now, Love, I have thee! I am he whom I love! . . ."

THE END

CPSIA information can be obtained
at www.ICGtesting.com
Printed in the USA
LVHW051519200921
698271LV00027B/1751